CU00858836

MILAN BIHLMANN & M. JAMMER YILMAZ

Milan Bihlmann is German, audacious, extroverted, sociable, and serene – all at the same time. He has the singular ability to begin each of his journeys with a treasure trove of unique experiences. Alongside his international commerce studies, he carried out a professional juggling career and became a Couch-Surfing ambassador.

Muammer Yilmaz is a humanist adventurer. Curious about the world, he cultivates a particular interest for people, cultures, and traditions… he already has many extraordinary voyages under his belt, across more than 70 countries. A director, photographer, drone pilot, and public speaker, he loves to launch new projects.

www.muammer.fr

AROUND THE WORLD
IN EIGHTY DAYS

Without money

EVERYTHING is
POSSIBLE

EVERYTHING IS
possible

MUAMMER YILMAZ
& MILAN BIHLMANN

in collaboration with Gaëlle Noémie Jan
translated by Kevin A. Castillo Montanye

AROUND THE WORLD IN EIGHTY DAYS

Without money

including a booklet of unpublished photos

Milan and Muammer

Two optimistic adventurers

MILAN

This journey could have started with nothing but his name. Milan's parents chose it after their encounter with a fascinating gypsy during one of their travels. He has proven them right, becoming a young citizen of the world. Audacious, extroverted, sociable, and serene, all at the same time, he has the singular ability to begin each of his journeys with a unique treasure trove of experiences: from a suit tailored to his measures by Fidel Castro's personal tailor to the organization of a joyful neighborhood party for underprivileged children in France, Milan has lived a little of everything.

In tandem with his studies in international commerce in Germany, France, and Canada, Milan carried out a professional juggling career and became a CouchSurfing ambassador. He loves partaking in all sorts of sports activities, knows how to entertain his friends with his storytelling skills, and is perpetually running projects.

Since his childhood in a tiny village of 146 people in Germany, he has kept his feet firmly on the ground and loves simple relationships. He conserves this attitude in foreign countries, whether it be in front of a horizon full of skyscrapers or a mindboggling canyon. He is a staunch believer in the curiosity of people and builds relationships with every individual who has an open heart and mind, as well as a good sense of humor.

In terms of globalization, his modest contributions to the construction of a peaceful world are creating multicultural encounters and uniting people of different religions and nationalities.

Milan knows very well that every adventure has its highs and its lows. Nonetheless, heeding the irresistible desire to constantly progress but also to explore his personal limits, he resolved to sell almost everything he owned in order to begin a new phase in his life by making a journey around the world without using any money.

MUAMMER

A curious adventurer who smiles at the world! Born in Colmar, Alsace, Muammer has always been full of positive energy. His first camera was given to him on his 17th birthday by his father, who wanted to congratulate him on his success at funding a trip to the United States himself. This was a gift that changed his life! In 2000, he founded TvCampus in Strasbourg, an association that takes charge of the formation of more than 500 students in the art of film directing and editing, opening the doors for them to journalism and audiovisual fields. Muammer loves sharing his passion and transmitting his energy to others. In 2005, he created the concept of the 48 Hour Video Marathon in Strasbourg.

A journalist, TV presenter, cameraman, editor, photographer, and radio host, Muammer is a jack of all trades. In 2008, he approached VIP Studio with the idea of conquering new creative territories. Today an independent director and photographer, Muammer is a travel enthusiast who loves collaborating with his friends worldwide in order to share images taken at the ends of the world. His last film, co-directed with Philippe Frey and coproduced by Alsace20, Les Peuples de l'Omo, was broadcast by the channel France 3-Alsace. Muammer has already made several extraordinary journeys, such as the one that saw him join a salt caravan in the middle of the desert in Chad, and allowed him to direct a documentary film: La Caravane noire.

With more than 400 trips across over 70 countries, Muammer is a globetrotter with endless amounts of faith in humanity. Curious about the world, he cultivates a particular interest in the people of the world, their cultural differences, their traditions, and their beliefs. He has an ambition to create encounters, to learn, and to enrich his life through these exchanges. To sum him up, he loves people, and among the values he holds dear to his heart are equality, tolerance, friendship, peace, and mutual respect between all people.

Brimming with positive energy and animated by the notion that everything is possible, Muammer is always on lookout for new challenges and projects. He loves cinema and the art of creating quality entertainment. This project, inspired by the famous novel written by the French author Jules Verne, reunites all of the ingredients that create a captivating scenario: encounters, adventure, dreams, sharing, and humanity!

Introduction

Two entities. Two paths. An encounter. A dream.

Two diametrically opposed entities. One is rational, the other effusive. One is adept at meditation, the other can't stay put. The roles seem predefined, and yet...

Two different paths: the first, atypical, combining a degree in international trade with performing arts and a command of juggling; the second, multidisciplinary, attached to images and with varied experience in direction, photography, and production. The roles are shared, and yet...

An encounter in the winter of 2010 in Berlin, Germany, which foretells a common future. Even though eleven years separate Milan Bihlmann and Muammer Yilmaz, and their respective areas of expertise are testament to their contradictory personalities, they decide to form a duo by the name of Optimistic Traveler (that is, to always be confident in the face of the future) in September of 2014, after only spending six days together since they've met. This duo leads to a fusion of visions and of ideas that are, contrary to their differences, complementary.

A dream, a crazy gamble, unites them like never before: the dream of traveling around the world in eighty days without money.

The author Jules Verne, and his literary creation Phileas Fogg[1], become anchored in Muammer's imagination from very early on, and he develops an irresistible attraction to the adventure of exploring faraway lands. Completing a round-the-world journey in eighty days? The idea is so tempting for him that it quickly seduces his partner.

During their previous travel experiences they faced many prejudices, both social and religious. They were however able to overcome these thanks to their encounters with different people who opened their hearts to the two travelers. This inspiration led them to the challenge that they were determined to undertake: to prove to the whole world that human beings are gifted with generosity and that they are destined to live in happiness.

The burgeoning project is a logical consequence of their surprising encounter. Milan, a Berlin-based ambassador for CouchSurfing[2], lodges Muammer for a weekend, and during this time, the link between the two and the base of this new friendship are formed. An insatiable need to travel, an attraction to cultural differences, and a worldly curiosity are the values that they share. Traveling is a given for them, but more than that, traveling differently, and with good measure: this race around the world, if feasible, is duty-bound to be well-motivated by their values.

---

1   Jules Verne: *Around The World in Eighty Days*
2   Founded in 2003, the social networking website 'Couchsurfing' provides a platform of hospitality services for members to stay as a guest at someone´s home, host travelers, meet other members, or join an event - without monetary exchange.

Optimistic Traveler and the 80 Days Challenge continue the lineage of adventurers passionate about alternative voyages, journeys guided by encounters where human warmth and generosity dismantle fears and prejudices. Antoine de Maximy from the French television show "J'irai dormir chez vous" ("I'll come sleep in your house") and Guillaume Mouton and Nan Thomassey from "Nus et Culottés" ("Naked and Daring"), are just a few of these such adventurers. With this spirit at heart, and for the sake of equality and a willingness to detach from all useless material properties, it was decided that this new adventure would be achieved without a single cent. After all, facing one's own needs seems to paradoxically be the key in opening one's self to others.

Thus, the Optimistic Traveler collaboration is born and the project is launched; a dream, a crazy challenge. With the constraints of the challenge established, the next step is to tackle its practical aspects. Since this adventure is but the first step on a path toward humanitarian work, media coverage and visibility is essential. To this effect, a website and pages on different social media platforms are set into action and are to be updated every day. After the press is informed, the first articles appear and the Internet community begins to respond – without a doubt, a precious support.

Other preparations need attention. Moving around without money requires finding another way to travel: hitchhiking. A test-run is essential when a beginner is honing a new skill; in this case, hitchhiking from Strasbourg to Berlin is the test. Can it be done? Thankfully, it is possible when one is obliged to ask others for help while adopting a respectful and positive approach. A new universe opens up, and the stories of the people who cross each other's paths give a new and captivating dimension to trips. These eighty days promise to be rewarding.

At the same time, the first questions and certain concerns appear. For example: will the principle of this adventure work? Will there be a place to sleep every day? Will certain countries, such as Pakistan or Iran, be as dangerous as people say? And will it be possible to cross the oceans?

Choosing equipment is not a small task. It is out of the question to travel around the world with heavy baggage that slows down the trip. A 30 liter capacity – around a dozen kilos – is more than enough in this case, however, certain essentials are required, such as a purifying water filter. In terms of wardrobe, only the strict minimum is allowed. After adding the digital nomad gear – cameras, a hard drive, and a laptop, among other objects – the backpacks are finally ready. One exception to the clothing rule is made: taking care of one's appearance allows encounters to be cultivated, and so a white shirt and a bowtie will be the trip's uniform, a sort of trump card just like Muammer's photographic talents and Milan's juggling abilities. One's charms and tools must be utilized to the fullest extent, and a diabolo and a camera lens are a good example of these, both disconcerting and enchanting.

Monday, September 8th, 2014. Paris, France. The clock ticks as the countdown is set in motion. The dream is at a fingertip, and the time to be thrown into reality is here...

Day 1 – Tuesday, September 9th, 2014
Paris – Strasbourg, France

Today is the grand departure. Countless days of preparation, of tests of all types – from hitchhiking training to backpack unloading in order to carry only the lightest of baggage – and of action plans, concerning the documentation for the voyage and the storage of pictures, have led us to this unmissable rendezvous.

9:09 AM

The hour has struck. On this morning of September 9th, 2014, we are here in Paris, at the foot of the Eiffel Tower: a threshold symbolic of our sizable test's beginning. Our challenge - that of making a voyage around the world in eighty days, without spending any money, with the purpose of exchanging, of helping, and of traveling without resorting to die-hard consumerism.

We exchange a look. "Are you ready to marry me for the next eighty days?" an amused Muammer asks me, and my frank "yes" resonates in response. I am well aware that this banter reflects the pact that we have just sealed and that we are now committed to the worst, as well as the best.

Today, when everything speeds up, we let ourselves be taken away by a whirlwind of emotions: the goodbyes with family and friends, the slight apprehension, and, most of all, the excitement. The thirst of discovering the world, of leaving to meet new people. Of breaking the rules, of surprising, of provoking, and of giving back – of traveling differently.

The Champ-de-Mars extends before us and majestic Paris spreads out its arms, and yet there is no time to lose if we want

15

to reach our objective for this first day: Strasbourg, 500 kilometers from here.

We enter a brewery in order to get a feel for the city. The mood inside is evident: everyone is busy. We too put our shoulder to the wheel – knowing how to slice shallots is a precious talent! – in exchange for a coffee shared with one of the cooks. Meanwhile, outside the brewery the race against time begins again. Cars, buses, and taxis speed by, their drivers in a hurry, busy, inattentive. The Parisian stress? We observe it in amusement but it holds no sway over us, and we can see that we aren't the only ones to hold this opinion in this brewery.

Guillaume, Julien, and their finance colleagues get ready to spend their lunch break having a picnic in the Champ-de-Mars, and they spontaneously invite us to join them and share their meal.

The adventure begins. Punctuated by light banter and more serious discussions, the gathering takes place and we nourish ourselves with this first real exchange. Our friends then offer us a tuk-tuk[3] to help us finally leave Paris. Happy to be able to begin our route, we take turns jumping onto our new steed heading toward a neighboring metro station. The Seine flows at our sides as we go along and the plant-covered wall of the musée du quai Branly gives us wings. Our eagerness at finally being able to begin our challenge acts up and the tuk-tuk unfortunately does not resist for a long time. Roussel, its owner, doesn't hold it against us...

According to our estimates, we need to travel at a pace of at least 300 kilometers per day in order to reach our final destina-

---

3   The 'Tuk-tuk' is the Thai nickname given to an auto-rickshaw, a three-wheeled miniature truck. In Paris, it is used for public transportation.

tion of Strasbourg. Leaving the capital is no small enterprise, but good vibes lead us forward and, thanks to the cooperation of Hafida who furnishes us with two public transport tickets, we reach the east of Paris. Then, in Bercy, our encounter with Kevin is decisive. This young father takes a detour, bringing us to the first gas station on the highway leading to Strasbourg. There, we endure a few rejections from passing drivers, until Azi helps us advance some kilometers, and Paul takes us to Reims. Paul, a medical student on his way to the grape harvest, exudes a good mood and he encourages us. His words, a mixture of carefreeness and wisdom, surprise us and go straight to our hearts. The surprises continue with Razak, who takes us to Metz. A man of Pakistani origin, Razak reassures us about the preconceptions of his country, and he offers simple and accurate advice about the possible outcome of our project: "It is important to remain humble and human." Our last surprise comes in the form of Bernard, our final driver who takes us to the foot of the Strasbourg Cathedral even though he has never picked up a hitchhiker before.

It is late when we arrive in Strasbourg, and we enjoy the autumnal ambiance. Around us, the full moon illuminates the little streets and outlines the half-timbered houses of the city. Groups of people pass us by, and some conversations begin but end rather quickly. Nonetheless, we continue to search for nourishment and lodging for the night.

Gina and Natalie's appearance was unexpected. The two well-dressed friends enjoying their evening with smiles on their lips are immediately interested in us. In a show of incredible open-mindedness, and an amiable trust in us, they take us out to eat and Gina graciously allows us to stay the night at her house.

The keys to our adventure have been well and truly given to us. We knew it beforehand but we now have the proof that our human encounters and exchanges will set the pattern for our trip and mark our path. Paris – Strasbourg, a first stage full of promise for the rest of the voyage.

Day 2 – Wednesday, September 10th, 2014
Strasbourg - Munich, Germany

Waking up to the sun at Gina's house in Strasbourg is a strange feeling for Muammer, who is from this city. Maneuvering in a familiar environment while staying within the constraints imposed by the Optimistic Traveler challenge is turning out to be difficult as we cannot utilize our contacts to find lodging or food. Nevertheless, our breakfast – coffees and croissants generously offered to us by the delicious bakery on the corner of the building – quickly cheers us up. There's nothing better than sharing a vision of happiness or a life philosophy to re-center and pacify one's spirits.

Gina, visibly stirred by our encounter, decides to go part of the way with us. Be it during radio and television interviews at our juggling and equilibristic performances in the park or during conversations with fruit, vegetable, and bread producers at the market while collecting supplies, Gina's calm strength and her generosity are unfailing gifts. Her presence is very precious to us.

The time to leave the city has come. By fate or coincidence, we quickly cross the path of Victoria, who in exchange for carefully cleaning her windshield, takes us to Kehl, Germany, just a few kilometers away.

The hitchhiking to Munich starts here.

At the wheel of the first car is Thomas, a rally amateur, who applies his passion to humanitarian work, most notably in Africa. In the second car, our driver is initially hesitant to talk but she eventually opens up a little and reveals that she used to be an actress. A mother and her daughter drive the third car, and though they are reserved about picking up perfect strangers, they nonetheless help us advance. The fourth and final car is driven by Michal, a salesperson, who kindly takes us to the center of Munich.

It is already late and the evening is well under way, but we cannot refuse an invitation from a group comprised of people of multiple nationalities to come join them in a Mexican restaurant in front of which we are standing. The cheerful ambiance surrounds us for hours, and even though we, unfortunately, still don't know where to sleep tonight, the help and encouragement of each one of our companions is valuable to us.

Midnight passed, we make haste to find lodging. The appearance of Marie, from France, and Miguel, from Switzerland, delivers us from our encroaching apprehension. After a long hesitation and some hemming and hawing, Marie accepts to host us in her room in the heart of a student residence. Due to the lack of permission to sleep in the building, we will be as discreet as possible in order to prevent problems for our hostess.

Strasbourg – Munich, a journey of 364 kilometers. We have won this gamble for our second day, though not without difficulties. The journey is full of refusals and is punctuated by long waits and reassessments. We are truly entering the heart of the matter, and the adventure is beginning. The excitement is present, and our curiosity takes us forward, however, we need to make adjustments. We cannot let ourselves be destabilized by certain negative behaviors or attitudes. We cannot burn too quickly through our energy, rather, we need to make sure to preserve it. We cannot expect anything, but only to let ourselves be surprised. We need to savor our encounters, be amazed at the diversity of profiles we cross, and finally, we need to smile while thinking about Gina's words: "My vision of happiness? Living the present moment and being in good company."

Day 3 – Thursday, September 11th, 2014
Munich – Linz, Austria

We spend an agitated night sleeping on the cold floor – evidently, the hazards of travel are slowly coming out of the woodwork. We have already fallen into a restrictive nightly routine of making sure to charge our cameras' batteries, finding water to filter, washing our socks and underwear, and then collecting our equipment and our clothing, often still damp, the next morning. However, waking up sheltered from the rain and the wind in a foreign city, thanks to the hospitality of young students, is nonetheless quite comforting. Up until now, at least, luck has been on our side, and we will take advantage of it to vigorously tackle this third day.

Our energy has a knack to flow in opposite directions. Traveling as a duo has imposed a certain rhythm, and functioning symbiotically requires some practice. We've decided to not argue about our differences in opinion about the strategy that we've created to continue on our path. Case in point: discovering Munich, its tourist spots, its parks, and strolling around fulfilling momentary desires; this is what perfectly suits Milan. On the other hand, I want to leave the city as soon as possible in order to not arrive too late to Vienna, today's destination.

Who is right? Who is wrong? There is none of that between us, and we compromise on everything, hoping that this will lead us to make good decisions, today and the next seventy-seven days. The important thing is to know how to always stay optimistic!

The cobblestone streets lead us the center of the city. The traditional Bavarian architecture, especially the churches, captures our attention, and the street musicians enchant our ears. However, it is the English Garden[4] where we spend our most positive moments of the day before continuing along.

Our everyday life now consists of finding the correct direction, stopping passing cars, speaking to the people inside to interest them in our adventure, adopting the right attitude, and finally plunging briefly into their private lives.

We also need to be patient, sometimes fate is on our side. One of these such instances, for example, was being picked up by Jonas, a young salesman with a passion for snowboarding and traveling. Jonas is one of those people who immediately opens his heart and his door (and that of his in-laws and their Asian restaurant, as it happens!), and who provide more than just assistance. It seems that open-mindedness and generosity will follow us in every region visited.

Nonetheless, our exchanges are sometimes more difficult: when the weather is anything but beautiful, when the wait is long, and when we realize that, once inside the car, we don't like the situation we've entered. Witnessing a violent couple's

---

4   The 'English Garden' or 'Englischer Garten' is one of the world´s largest urban public parks, larger than New York´s Central Park and London´s Hyde Park.

argument or making our drivers uneasy are just some of the situations that aren't pleasant and that make us uncomfortable.

Sometimes, even though we don't give up easily, we regretfully have to find another car to ride in.

We don't reach Vienna this night, and we set down our backpacks in Linz. Our day has been punctuated by disagreements and failure, but none of that matters; every moment shared together stays in our memory. The names parade, one after another, in our minds: Maria, Miguel, Jonas, Anna, Irina, Ali, Harun, Habib... each of their stories, at times more complex than we could have imagined, mark us deeply. We gather their confidences as symbols of their trust. Their revelations touch us; they destabilize us. The language barrier, sometimes more than others, acts as a filter, and Milan, who speaks German, is today a direct witness to these deeply moving confessions. Our emotions reach a high point, and our challenge takes on a new dimension.

We pass from one life to another, just as we pass from one car to another. We feel humility in the face of these glimpses into new perspectives.

We are definitely traveling in a different manner, and now more than ever we are impatient to discover what the future has in store for us.

Day 4 – Friday, September 12th, 2014
Linz – Budapest, Hungary

One night in the Optimistic Traveler adventure is also a voyage into the heart of foreign cultures. Tonight we find ourselves in Linz, Austria, but it is Afghanistan that we are visiting instead, thanks to our hosts.

Harun, Ali, and Habib share an apartment and a turbulent past. Habib, a former translator and interpreter for the United States Army in Afghanistan, had to leave his country for safety reasons, and spent a significant amount of money to do so, which has led to an uncertain financial and professional future. Ali and Harun also had a long and exhausting journey before arriving in Linz, yet neither of them are lacking in joie-de-vivre and hospitality. We have barely woken up when Ali invites us to eat breakfast in the living room, and we enjoy this pleasant moment while sitting on the rug. As if he hadn't already done enough for us, Ali also drives us to the first gas station on the highway leading to Budapest, and doesn't leave us until after we share a last coffee and he's sure that another driver has picked us up.

Our journey continues eastward to Vienna in the company of Rebeka and Laurentiu, both Romanian, and our positive and enthusiastic state of mind light up our day's travels.

When we find a new car to ride in, we take advantage of the opportunity to share our love for music and spectacles, juggling included, with a group of hitchhikers heading to a festival, and we realize, once again, that our values and our opinions are shared with many people that we meet on the road. We talk about this with Ali, from Turkey, and Karina, from Hungary, with whom we spend a few hours on the way to Budapest. Our exchanges and shared stories are an important wealth to preserve.

For the first time since our departure, we arrive at our destination in the afternoon while it is still light out. It is 5 o'clock in Budapest, Hungary, and the city unveils to us its charm, its architecture, and its treasures. The sun sets behind the Danube and puts on a magical show. At the last glimmers of the day, we meet Philippe, who contacted us on social media. Captivated by our project and attentive to our journey, he has decided to help us during our passage through the Hungarian capital with the assistance of one of his friends. Together, we drive around the city, we have dinner on the terrace of a Kurdish restaurant, and we go out at night in an animated neighborhood. Spending time in this city is quite nice, especially when we are guided by the goodwill and generosity of people that were strangers mere hours ago.

Even more kind gestures come our way: Philippe, passing in front of a grocery, decides to buy us supplies so that we have all we need to have breakfast the next morning. Hervé, his friend, gives us the keys to his apartment for the night. A whole apartment just for us... unbelievable! And stocked with a washing machine, no less? We seem to be living a dream!

Fourth day on the road. We have experienced human warmth and positive energies, and the comfort of housing; Optimistic Traveler is born under a lucky star.

Day 5 – Saturday, September 13th, 2014
Budapest – Border of Romania

Well-rested, we enjoy the morning alongside Philippe and his young children. Our complicity and the laughs shared with them during my diabolo juggling demonstrations recharge our batteries. We meet Hervé and his daughter for a coffee, taking the advantage of thanking him once again for his hospitality.

Philippe, however, isn't yet done with us. Delighted to be able to show us Budapest, his adoptive city for over twenty years, he doesn't miss a single sight. We take a walk, enjoying

24

each place as we go, from the banks of the Danube next to the Hungarian Parliament Building to an abandoned building, home to graffiti artists, ending up at the Heroes' Square. We finally leave the city after one last pause at a café where the atmosphere evokes that of Viennese cafés. Philippe, wanting us to be able to hitchhike easily, drops us off at a service station on the highway leading to Belgrade. This is a good idea that comes to an abrupt end.

It's not the multiple refusals that modify our plan; it is the reaction of the employees of the service station that quickly makes us decide to do something else. Put off by our demeanor and our constantly brandished camera, they promptly call the police – a delicate gesture that makes us run for our lives! Luckily Philippe was still in the vicinity, and he helps us avoid this unfortunate event and takes us to the next station.

Here, circulation is less frequent, and we head toward a nearby Turkish restaurant. Inside, we are in another world: the world of truck drivers. We strike up conversations and make negotiations, and we receive an unexpected response. Aytaç agrees to give us a ride, "at our own risk". Once we are in his truck, we understand what he means by this: with more than 700,000 kilometers on the odometer, the engine could eventually decide to stop at any moment. This doesn't happen immediately, though, and we depart.

Sitting on the bench behind the seats, I take advantage of the moment to rest. It is my turn to discover the difficulties of the language barrier that is becoming commonplace in our journey, and in this case, brought about by our encounter with Turkish. Even though we both play the role of interpreter from time to time, exclusion is inevitable at certain moments.

25

During this time, Muammer animatedly talks to our driver in Turkish. Aytaç shares details about his life as a truck driver and tells us stories about frequent bribes with the policemen of the region. The atmosphere is positive and we can imagine traveling with him for the rest of the 900 kilometers between us and Istanbul.

Another good idea that ends abruptly. Things quickly go south when the police stop the truck for a vehicle identification check. Under heavy rain, we are escorted to the place where Aytaç, in bad shape and guilt-laden, must pay a fine of 600 euros and must impound his vehicle during two days.

It is dark out and, wet to the bone, we cross the Hungary-Romania border on foot. We recover our precious passports after an hour wait and many doubts. Knowing that our passports were in the hands of strangers raised our fears of seeing the challenge reduced to nothing due to a problem with our papers. It definitely isn't recommended to film here since the police is never far away, and our difficulties with the Romanian language don't help us communicate.

As the hours pass, our fatigue manifests itself, as well our impatience. We have only a few options: find lodging for the night, sleep uncomfortably in Aytaç's impounded vehicle, or simply continue along our route...

Day 6 – Sunday, September 14th, 2014
Border of Romania – Bucharest, Romania

During the night, our troubles come to an end. After a few sketchy encounters that didn't promise to end well, luck once again was on our side and we headed toward Bucharest with a Romanian couple, Nicu and Catalina.

Nicu is a sociologist of gypsy origins. His latest research culminated in a documentary about Romanian emigration and the confrontation between myth and reality in this situation, which to him seems more like a form of deportation. Our enriching exchanges take place throughout the night, interspersed with extraordinary episodes where we struggled to find our path after several detours.

The voyage continues. The route is long, and the night seems endless, but in the early hours of the morning the light finally chases away the darkness. We take several breaks along the way in order to allow our driver to rest, and a good mood keeps us company. The industrial landscapes, often abandoned, are constant along the drive. The sun rises slowly in the sky, and the Romanian fields and nature re-establish their dominion over the factories. After a last nap on the grass, we finally reach our destination, Bucharest.

The outskirts of the city are littered with the vestiges of the communist era, but when we reach the center, we discover many architectural treasures in the streets of Bucharest, including buildings fashioned after the Art Nouveau or Bauhaus styles.

Nicu and Catalina drop us off close to a large welcoming avenue. Several minutes go by before we see a car arrive and park near us. Inside the vehicle there are two affable young people who invite us to have a coffee with them. While sitting in a large terrace, our photographic equipment catches the eye of two amateurs who strike up a conversation with us and offer us drinks. Later on, it is the Turkish community who shows us their hospitality. Without even accepting our propositions to work in exchange for some food, the owner of a restaurant in which we stop at offers us a complimentary and delicious meal. It is a complete and warm meal, our first after 24 hours!

Afterwards, we encounter Aurélien, a French professor and philosophy enthusiast, who guides us to a youth hostel, The Little Bucharest. Luanna greets us when we arrive, but the possibility of leaving our backpacks there for the night is uncertain. She nonetheless gains the approval of her supervisor, and we rejoice in the face of this good fortune.

While walking around the hallways and outside of the hostel we quickly make new acquaintances. One such person, a Frenchman, is a magician and photographer who also travels the world to offer magic shows to underprivileged children; a beautiful story.

In the evening, the neighboring plaza hosts a street festival. The music resonates, and the ambiance transports us; Milan needs no invitation and dives into the festivities with a wild diabolo performance. Accompanied by the sweet notes of a flute and a piano, he flawlessly executes a choreography that quickly captivates the crowd. Our adventure is shared by the festival host who passes the microphone to Milan, and we are invited to dinner by Gilbert, a passionate spectator. We graciously accept his invitation in the spirit of privileging our face-to-face exchanges.

After a full evening, we return to the hostel to go to sleep for the night. The kilometers of our journey do not rest, and we shall resume our challenge at a good time tomorrow morning.

Day 7 – Monday, September 15th, 2014
Bucharest, Romania – Istanbul, Turkey

As planned, in the morning we leave the hostel with Goran to have breakfast. We spend a part of the morning together, and later desire to continue along our route.

Which direction should we take to leave the city? Should we go south? Or to the east? We tentatively search for the right way, but quickly realize that our confusion about the map of Europe at the beginning of our trip and a preparation of an itinerary are a waste of time because each day we must obtain our answers from the locals. We can't say we weren't warned!

By pure luck, our roaming lead us straight to the aptly-named Istanbul restaurant. We see a sign and we enter the establishment. Nihat, a customer, sits us down in front of a tea and he announces that he will accompany us to a station. We make a quick stop at his apartment a little bit later and we arrive, not to the bus station, but to a residential and garage building. After Nihat recounts our story, his friend Mehmet, the owner of the place, and his colleague promise to help us. They are not in a hurry, though, since the next departure to Istanbul isn't until a few hours from now. Every setback can be painted in a positive light, and we spend these few hours with this joyful community, playing soccer in a nearby park and sharing a meal. Evidently, hospitality and sharing continue to color our experience.

When we finally arrive at the bus station, our new friends buy us a ticket, and the owner of the bus company buys us the second. It is now official: we are departing for Turkey. The emotion is overwhelming, and we don't know what to say in the face of such generosity. We effusively thank our benefactors and we climb aboard the bus.

Bucharest slowly fades away behind our backs. The sunset clears up our route, and we rapidly get accustomed to the bumpy rhythm of bus travel. Multiple stops punctuate our progress, and we take advantage of these to initiate a conversation with one of our neighbors, Julius. Once the bus sets off again, we first travel across Bulgaria, and then, in the middle of the night, we finally arrive at the much-anticipated border post.

Turkey.

Day 8 – Tuesday, September 16th, 2014
Istanbul, Turkey

At 3 o'clock in the morning, we disembark to explore Istanbul. I can't stop myself from telling Milan that this is, for me, the most beautiful city in the world. Nonetheless, this excitement at beginning a new stage in our journey disappears as quickly as it arrived: just a few minutes off the bus to refresh ourselves are enough for a person with ill intentions to search our backpacks and take off with a valuable loot. The result: we are down one camera, two lens, one flash, and some batteries. Our equipment has taken a hit, and so has our morale.

We spend several hours collecting witness statements from the driver and the passengers, with Julius's account being, notably, crucial. Afterwards, we go to a police station to compose our statements. This doesn't particularly help speed up the process and instead leads to some tension between us and the police officers. However, the feeling ends up dissipating and giving place to light banter and good humor. This is how we manage, at 5 in the morning, to get a photo with Turkish policemen!

Our resentment at this unexpected moment passes, and the adventure must continue. Who doesn't have in their repertoire travel stories like this? At least, we can say that our arrival in Istanbul did not go by unnoticed.

The sun is finally up. The weather is beautiful, and our strolls around the Blue Mosque, the Hagia Sophia, and its gardens are like a gentle balm on our hearts. In the spirit of boosting our legendary optimism, we ask some high school students to assign us a challenge for the day, and their proposition is quick to come: we must try to sleep in a luxury hotel for free. We take up their challenge with glee.

A transformation takes place: a white shirt and a bow tie are our tools to help us with our objective. The first hotel in which we present ourselves offers us a surprisingly warm reception, but the hostess can't make any promises without her manager's approval. Second try: the Hotel Armada, a four-star establishment. The discussion extends over several minutes, and they offer us fruit juice. Suddenly, the receptionist grants us a comfortable and well-appointed room and leads us to the breakfast hall where a simple glimpse of the buffet table is enough to make our mouths water.

We take advantage of the calm environment to recover from the night spent on the bus and to respond to several media outlets that have contacted us. At the end of the afternoon we leave the hotel to explore the jumble of alleys of the Sultanahmet neighborhood where we are staying. We savor the Istanbul way of life, drink tea in a hammam, and get our beards trimmed at an old barber's shop. All of this, of course, is thanks to the generosity and sympathy of the people we are lucky to meet and who ceaselessly offer us some Turkish wisdom: "her sey para deyil", which literally means "money isn't everything".

Once the night arrives, the cosmopolitan tourist neighborhood is even livelier. The restaurants are constantly packed with people and, even though we don't find a meal for the night, a vendor offers us cones of chocolate and vanilla ice cream after a memorable show of magical dexterity. We have something to calm our hunger and we go to sleep tonight with beautiful memories fresh in our minds.

FROM
EUROPE
TO
TURKEY

8 DAYS = 3 008KM

GERMANY

Strasbourg

Linz

Paris

FRANCE

Munich AUSTRIA HUNGARY

Budapest

ROMANIA

Bukarest

Istanbul

TURKEY

Day 9 – Wednesday, September 17th, 2014
Istanbul – Ankara, Turkey

Relaxed and refreshed, we recommence our journey in this Eastern land. We stop to thank Nedim at the reception one last time, and then we head to the port. Thanks to some young Dutch people, we board the ferry heading to the Anatolian Peninsula. As we leave the waters of the Bosphorus, the Galata Tower, a vestige of the Eighteenth Century, bids us goodbye. We are now sailing across the Sea of Marmara, leaving Europe behind us.

Our goal for today is to reach Ankara, the capital city of Turkey, by tonight, even though it is 450 kilometers away. We commence our scouting and ask around the minute we arrive on the bridge. Unfortunately, nobody has planned to undertake this long route. Once we arrive on the dock, it is the same tune. Some drivers gladly offer us tea and doughnuts, but we don't get anywhere, and we find it difficult to leave the city. Suddenly, we see an old but gleaming blue Volkswagen Beetle approach us. Inside, a young and smiling couple agree to pick us up and take us a little farther on the highway toward Ankara.

Once the car has dropped us off on the roadside, things get complicated. The highway is a hive of activity, but it seems hard to stop a car. We somehow manage to reach a nearby gas station, where we negotiate in vain with a bus company who has a stop there, and we finally enter a small restaurant. There, our encounter with Yahya, married father of two and a truck driver for over twelve years, changes the course of our day. Delighted, we take up our route with him, who has never picked up hitchhikers before.

The rhythm recommences. The asphalt extends all the way to the horizon. We drive along the coast, and the cargo ships punctuate the seascape. The time goes by slowly, and we we each take turns resting on the seat. Night falls and brings along with it some rain. Toward 10 at night, we arrive at a rest stop. We are still two or three hours away from Ankara, but it is here where our path diverges from Yahya's.

Before setting off again, he shares a word or two with the owner of the restaurant and a couple fellow truck drivers. His first experience with hitchhikers seems to have pleased him, and if he can help us find a new car he would be reassured. The task is, nonetheless, a bit more delicate than he had anticipated. Gürhan offers us a meal in his establishmnet but the other truck drivers leave without us.

Will we be able to arrive in Ankara before the sunrise?

Day 10 – Thursday, September 18th, 2014
Ankara – Göreme, Turkey

Sahaddetin saves us from a night at the rest stop, and at around 1 in the morning we are finally on our way toward Ankara on his truck. He spontaneously opens up his extremely neat truck cab and, at the same time, opens his private space to us. Sahaddetin does not talk much, as he prefers to concentrate on the drive. In turns, we sleep on a comfortable mattress that serves as guest bed behind the seats, hidden by a thick curtain.

We advance in the darkness. Sahaddetin is in a hurry to reach Ankara, where he is expected. We accompany him to the delivery address of his cargo. We take advantage of the occasion to help him in return for his generosity by unloading dairy products and ayran[5] from the truck to the warehouse. Sahaddetin then lets us off in the outskirts of the sleeping city. Lost in the dark maze of avenues, we are guided in the right direction by several taxi drivers who drive us for free. Based on their advice, we head to the Kocatepe Mosque. It is 5 in the morning, and we push against the big door, enter the building and immediately go to sleep on the rugs for only three or four hours.

Our awakening is almost unreal as we discover the place in the daylight. The colossal pillar, the colored mosaics, and the hypnotizing interlacing make us feel bewitched and contemplative at the same time. We spend the morning continuing to discover the city. We take our time and we stroll between the fruit stands, the bakeries, the cafés, and the newsstands. We cannot miss visiting the impressive Anitkabir Mausoleum, built in honor of the founder and first president of the Turkish Republic, Mustafa Kemal Atatürk. We pause for a short while on the roof of the museum to observe Ankara's cityscape and then we continue our journey.

Step by step, from one space to another like in a board game, we manage to leave the city. A first car takes us to a service station, and a second takes us a little farther, where a bus picks us up and drops us off at the next station. Here, we approach customers and find our chance card: Nesrin, captivated by our trip around the world, gives Muammer the contact information of one of her friends who lives in Uçhisar, in Cappadocia, and I find Mohammed and Asker who immediately accept to take us on board their sedan. We aren't only assured to advance many kilometers today but we also have an opportunity for lodging for the night. Optimism pays off!

---

5   Recipe for 2 big glasses: 15 cl of goat´s or sheep´s yogurt, 30 cl water, 1 pinch of salt. Pour in a mixer, stir for some seconds until the mixture is creamy. Serve chilled!

We drive at a brisk pace in the direction of Adana with our new companions. Of Chechen origin, they don't speak a single word of Turkish, English, or any of the other three languages that we have at our disposal, and yet, thanks to a clever app on their smartphone which instantly translates what we say, we manage to communicate. Here is the benefit of new technologies! It is through this means of expression that our improbably encounter takes place: "How can I help you, my friend?" The robotic voice still resonates in our ears, and the surprise is complete.

In a show of faultless generosity, they invite us for lunch. The cellphone passes from hand to hand and, to our surprise, we soon find ourselves plunged into this out-of-the-ordinary communication system. We once again continue our route where the fields around us extend in every direction and the mountains cut the horizon. We stop for a while at the shores of Lake Tuz, its saltwater evaporating in the heat of the season as we advance delicately over this stretch of sand with its mirage-like qualities. The luminosity of the lake is blinding, and the emotion of the moment invades us.

However, our emotion comes to a peak when Asker and Mohammed announce to us that they're willing to make a 150-kilometer detour to take us to our meeting point in Göreme, and we cannot believe our good fortune.

This is how we find ourselves in Cappadocia seated, with our friends, around sumptuous Turkish specialties. The app on their phone works on overtime. We get to know each other, and we curiously ask them why they are so generous with us. They respond:

"We are believers and, for us, it is imperative to help our fellow human beings. If a person on our route needs assistance, we aren't going to leave them on their own." All of this before adding: "You are definitely the most interesting and captivating travel companions that we have been blessed to meet."

This has been a wonderful encounter and rich exchange for us, as well. Profound, simple, and magical.

Asli, Nesrin's friend, joins us at this moment. Her dynamism and her friendliness are immediately fetching. Asker and Mohammed need no more proof that we are in good hands, and they can leave with calm spirits. This is just one more detail that touches us and makes us smile. They do not leave without making us promise to keep in touch, and we cannot imagine thinking differently!

We watch them pull away and we continue our conversation with Asli. We appreciate her company, as well as her friend Ali's, for the rest of the evening. We feel tired now, and we go to the room that she has graciously reserved for us in her hotel, the Hotel Kelebek.

Our day ends as peacefully as it began in the heart of the mosque.

Day 11 – Friday, September 19th, 2014
Göreme – Elaziğ, Turkey

We wake up at the break of dawn with an idea in our heads. If we're going to follow in the footsteps of Jules Verne and Phileas Fogg, then we must go all the way.

We arrive at the meeting place of the Skyway Company while the moon is still shining in the sky. It's barely 5 in the morning and there is already a crowd here. Alper, the supervisor on duty, promises that he'll do as much as possible, but nothing is for sure. And indeed, we spend part of the night searching for a spot but, even though there are hundreds of hot-air balloons setting off each day, our efforts are in vain. We have faith in our lucky stars, though, and we still go to the company. This turns out to be a good decision because a sick person doesn't show up, leaving us a spot to access one of the dreams we have in common – that of sailing around the skies in a hot-air balloon. Just the idea of being able to fulfill this dream creates a tornado of emotions inside us, but how are we going to decide who is going to take that spot? We decide to leave it up to fate or to chance. I choose tails; Muammer heads. The coin spins in the air, and then falls on the ground. The verdict is...

Tails.

I board the vessel and take my spot in the basket. At each propulsion of the flame, the hot air inflates the canvas balloon and the vessel rises up higher. The hot-air balloon flies over the Göreme National Park, almost grazing the eroded reliefs and the tent rocks.

The sun is rising and the landscape is magnificent. The multitude of multicolored balloons contrasts this rocky décor, which is satisfying and calming in its immensity. We continue this ballet for almost an hour before returning to the ground, and to reality. Here, we need to tame the canvas monsters, a delicate operation. Reunited on the ground, we reform our duo.

I talk about my impressions, and then we join Ali who had hosted us in the city. We wander his ancestral lands on board his tractor, before reaching a veritable oasis in the heart of some troglodyte dwellings; his little paradise in which he'd like to grow old, he confesses. Underneath lush green vegetation, we share breakfast: fresh and dried fruit, vegetables, cheese, and honey, all accompanied by a steaming tea. A true delight to the senses, and truly memorable moments in Cappadocia.

We thanks our hosts, wave goodbye to the other travelers also present, and we kick up some dust. The challenge is above everything, so we continue along our path.

Once again alone, we're plunged in doubt. The waiting and incertitude certainly come in pairs. We board many vehicles but we advance at a snail's pace. First, a tractor takes us outside Göreme where, to our great surprise, a police car helps us out. Afterwards, we are saved from the crossroads we are stranded in by Ozkan, a truck driver. We discover inside the truck a surprising cab personality. Red curtains, felt flowers, plushy keychains; obviously, the decoration hasn't been left to one side! We ride with him until we reach Kayseri, all the while being surrounded by the beats of Turkish music.

We must wait, yet again, and this time we are tired. There's not much space on the side of the road, and vehicles pass by very rarely. Mehmet and his concrete cargo drop us off at the exit of the city, where Ayhan picks us up to then drop us off at a service station. Our hitchhiking is not successful here, and we barely catch a second car to go to the next station. The impatience and frustration grow by the second.

We are delivered from this by Muharrem's appearance. He is heading to Elazığ, 450 kilometers from here. It's not even necessary to say that we jumped for joy upon hearing the good news. The long journey is punctuated by laughs and confessions. He tells us about his Kurdish origins, about his beliefs, and reminds us that equality is the most beautiful of values, even if the world has the tendency to forget this. This is a message that we can't help but approve of.

Our paths diverge at Elaziğ. Shortly thereafter, we cross another path, Emrah's. We begin our discussion with him and he quickly offers us a place to stay. Though we are doubtful due to the rapidity of his proposition, we decide to nonetheless follow him. After a long walk, we reach his apartment and we meet his friends and roommates, Muhammet, Yusuf, and Hüseyin. Here, we learn to trust destiny, because the hospitality is immediately evident, and the friends make us feel like we're at home after the very first few seconds. The ambiance is relaxed, and the end of the evening cheerful.

Our adventure fills us day by day. The surprises and the magic we witness in the different places and events we live transport us entirely.

Day 12 – Saturday, September 20th, 2014
Elaziğ - Muş, Turkey

This morning our good spirits are in full swing. Everyone is ready, and we travel by car to Harput, the ancient historical city of which Elaziğ is an extension. From the top of the mountain, on top of the fortification, we overlook the valley. On the sunny terrace, we enjoy a traditional Turkish breakfast of different cheeses and olives, and we enjoy the genuine moment of sharing with our companions. This exchange, like all the ones that have come before during our adventure, is important to us. However, what is the most surprising and pleasing to us is the fact that our hosts are also immensely enjoying this rare occasion to spend time together.

Their origins are definitely different – the historical conflict that pits Turks and Kurds against each other is still present in their minds, even if their mentalities have evolved – but they are no less equal to each other and remain human above everything. Their fraternity is beautiful to witness, and their smiles shatter all prejudices.

Reluctantly we must leave once more as we go to Elazığ's bus station. Emrah, Muhammet, and Hüseyin are ready to buy us tickets, a proposition that we cannot refuse, but since the departure to Van, the next city, isn't until 10 at night, we decide to hitchhike instead. Our optimism is ever present.

We take up our strategic post at the service station on the outskirts of the city, and we cross our fingers that our lucky stars don't abandon us at this point. The heat is overwhelming, and the wind is kicking up dust clouds. Cars are very, very rare, but a truck suddenly passes by and Muammer jumps up to flag it down. The driver on board, a young man, immediately accepts to drive us for the next 150 kilometers. A first stage.

We advance very slowly due to the cargo of 52 tons of metal. We take advantage of the opportunity to admire the craggy landscapes; we enjoy this too much, probably, because the vehicle breaks down and stands us for a while in this magnificent landscape. A little bit of elbow grease, and we're off once more until the next interruption. We decide then to change vehicles and we meet Yunus, a Muslim Kurdish grandfather who invites us into his truck's cab. Delighted to be able to share this part of his trip with someone, he tells us about his life and anecdotes about his multiple drives. The sun begins to descend in the sky and the golden light guides us across the mountains.

We stop in a small village 30 kilometers away from Muş to unload the sacks of animal feed that Yunus is transporting. We help him out and catch the eye of the young people of the village. We share a meal with Yunus, still under the watchful gaze of the locals. Fascinated by the camera, the children direct their attention to me as soon as I draw my diabolo. With this gesture, an immediate connection is established with the

42

village people. All possible fears are dissipated, and the trust and good intentions are obvious, laughter in the air. My show delights the locals and they ask for an encore; art shows its power and breaks down the barriers.

Night has fallen, and it is time to continue the journey. Shortly we arrive in the animated center of Muş, thanks to a kind taxi driver. We walk a little and join a group of young people sitting around a steaming teapot. When we tell them about our search for lodging, they good-naturedly point out the teacher's house, not far from here, and they invite us to follow them. After a short walk, we reach the residence. We introduce ourselves, still accompanied by our guides, to the receptionist. Our adventure interests the manager, who is sorry that he cannot offer us a room due to a conference which has left him with no vacancy. However, he proposes that we can sleep on mattresses in the prayer room, and we accept the offer immediately.

Our story spreads in the residence hall and the young professors, intrigued by our adventure, soon invite us to go out again for some tea. Seated at a terrace, we share our experiences and we learn from each other.

The good surprises haven't stopped coloring our path across Turkey and contradict all of the warnings we had, especially about our safety. The freedom of thinking and of acting, and the open-mindedness that we have experienced in our lives are the most precious thing we have encountered, and tonight, surrounded by new acquaintances, we once again have proof that these values are universal.

Day 13 – Sunday, September 21st, 2014
Muş – Ahlat, Turkey

We join the same group of people in the breakfast hall the next morning. Discussions are quickly struck up, and prove diverse; our energy is infectious. Recep joins us, with a smile on his face, and offers us a package. Inside is a T-shirt that he wishes to see in New Delhi in a few days. We make a promise: we will send him a photograph of one of us wearing his gift in the streets of the Indian capital. His eyes shine with delight at our promise.

A minibus drops us off on the outskirts of the city, and we quickly set up to flag the vehicles that pass us by on the road. By necessity, we have adjusted to this different sort of everyday life, but the wait still seems endless. A car driving in the opposite sense curiously stops near us and turns around. The driver and his passenger, intrigued by our presence on the side of the road, get out of the car and join us. After a short exchange with them, they invite us into their car and propose that we go with them to a wedding happening in the small neighboring village of Altinova. The invitation is one of the most serious that we have received so far because it comes directly from the mayor; what a chance encounter!

Dressed in white shirts and bowties, we follow Mehmet Suat to the place where the event is taking place. From the town hall to the garden of someone's home, the celebration is in full swing, and he proudly introduces us to everyone. The entire village of about 500 people seems to be present for the occasion, men on one side and women on the other. We observe these scenes and we take part in the festivities, happy that this journey has allowed us to experience and enjoy such a wonderful opportunity.

A truck makes its entrance, carrying great pots of food in the back. A human chain forms, and plates soon pass from hand to hand and cover the long tables set out for the meal. The notes of traditional music and chants rise up over the crowd, and everyone's moods are high. The older people's faces are marked; the younger people's laughing. Our presence at the celebration surprises, bringing up curious questions.

Suddenly, the mood rises effervescently as the bride joins her groom. Firecrackers are set off everywhere, and children run crying in delight. It is now the mayor's turn to introduce Milan, who kicks off the show with his juggling and acrobatic skills. The endless pairs of eyes in the crowd do not leave the diabolo once. The people, with bated breath, observe the show and soon erupt into admiring cheers. The experience, rather different from what we've lived before, is incredible for each of us.

Nonetheless, we must leave once more. Mehmet accompanies us until the exit of Altinova, and we brusquely pass from a festive environment where the spirits were high to a complete and empty silence. Here, on the side of the road, there is not a single soul. We are alone in the middle of nowhere, and we feel a big wave of loneliness. It is a strange sensation, recurrent since the beginning of the trip, that shakes us. It is an impression that comes and goes in a constant back-and-forth. Walking, dancing, and taking photos... we utilize every means possible to distract ourselves and to attract the attention of potential drivers.

Hakki is the first to help us out. He takes us in his van to Tatyan, on the shores of Lake Van. Here we are overwhelmed by uncertainty as we cannot find a new car to ride in and the people we cross rarely know the way to Iran. We advance blindly.

In total, six cars pick us up for short stretches, and the end of the day is still not in sight. Finally, Adnan drives us to Ahlat. The parking lot of the restaurant he drops us off at is full of people, and we try to find a truck to drive us through the night in order to make up some of the kilometers that we've lost today. Alas, the road is cut off and no one can leave. Ismaïl and Faruk generously invite us into their establishments, where the environment is calm and agreeable. We soon share our experiences with the people gathered there, and Faruk soon takes us into a room where he feeds us like we've never been fed before, before taking us to another room where we will sleep. We have overlaid mattresses, and only basic accommodations, but we nonetheless have a roof under which we can sleep tonight.

Day 14 – Monday, September 22nd, 2014
Ahlat, Turkey

The sun rises over the Middle-East and, with it, new questions. Milan has spent an agitated night, full of vomiting and diarrhea. For the first time during our adventure, we cannot move forward due to health issues. These are difficulties that are beyond us and against which moral and mental strength can't fight. Our challenge is closely tied to our physical strength and if one of us isn't in top form, our dynamic is altered.

Bedridden for the entire day, Milan tries to somehow recover. During this time, I offer Faruk my help to clean the car and doing some errands, all to thank him for the lodging he has provided us, and also as a way to keep the challenge going in the face of this unforeseen pause.

Milan manages to slowly get up in the afternoon, just as multiple trucks begin to drive by in the small city. Dayut, a truck driver setting off for Tehran, accepts to drive us. Luck-

46

ily, the departure is pushed back to the evening in order to wait for his uncle and brother-in-law, a short delay that allows Milan to regain his strength while lounging first on the grass and then in the cargo area of the truck.

The sun sets over the shores of Van Lake. It has been another day spent underneath the Turkish sun, a stage which is currently at a standstill. Our patience is being sorely tested... for good reason, we're sure. We recommence our route in the middle of the dark night. Each of us riding in a different truck, we begin our nerve-racking mountain crossing.

Days 15 to 23 – from Tuesday, September 23nd, to Wednesday, October 1st, 2014
Ahlat, Turkey – Tehran, Iran

Twenty-third day of the adventure. The metal gates of the border post appear at the end of the paved road. We leave our driver and walk the rest of the way. We pass by the doors and validate our entry into this new territory. We're on the other side, in Iran, finally.

But first, let's go back a little bit:

Fifteenth day of the adventure. The night has been long on the bus. Dayut, ever attentive, asks us upon our awakening if we weren't cold on the bus. He offers us some breakfast that we share with other truck drivers at a rest stop and then we continue along our journey. Still in different trucks, we amuse ourselves with our drivers by trying to pass each other on the road. The environment is beautiful: the rising sun pierces the clouds, and the arid mountains surround us. We are almost at our goal for the day, the border post of Gürbulak is there, right in front of us. Our excitement is palpable.

Unfortunately, we only see Iran from across its gates. An organization error forces us to change our plans: Milan, traveling with his German passport, doesn't have the required visa to enter the country. Our disappointment is immense, but we try to stay positive. The Turkish policemen are, in this moment, a great help to us. They are going to help us convincing the Iranian authorities to provide us with a visa-on-arrival, an operation that is carried out in vain but is well-appreciated. Ersin lets us rest in his office and provides us with food and drinks. After inquiring about the requirements at the border, we must travel to the city of Erzurum to go to the Iranian Embassy. Our new friend spreads the news and neither he nor his colleagues allow a car to go by without learning of their destination. Finally, Basri saves us from a long wait, and mounting agony, by accepting to drive us to our destination.

A few hours later, we reach Erzurum. Night has fallen, and we must still gather our energy in order to find a place to stay for the night. We ask many people, but none of them accept to host us, so we continue to wander through the streets of the city until we cross a young man who saves us after a long string of refusals. Bahattin, concerned about his fellow man, immediately tells us to follow him. Thanks to his goodwill, we spend the night in the Muslim community of the "Nurcu", hosted by Muhammet, happy and relieved to have found a shelter after this long and tough day.

Beginning the following morning we tackle the task of fulfilling the formalities to obtain the precious visa, but nothing goes as expected. The news reaches our ears like a harsh sentence: the period needed to obtain the visa is much longer than we had thought, and so we're stuck in Erzurum.

The challenge is now in the hands of the administration, and we are completely uncertain about our immediate future.

The emotions we feel are difficult to deal with in the face of this new ordeal, even though we have no one to blame but ourselves. We fall down and we allow ourselves to cry together. During the days, five in total, we stay stranded here, we pass through all of the stages: worry, distress, sadness, guilt, exasperation, enthusiasm, and euphoria. A veritable rollercoaster, indeed. However, the novelty of the adventure is still present. Faced with the unknown and, unlike before, now no longer the masters of our adventure, we experience the journey in a different but still enriching manner.

Our encounters with different people are the constant backdrop of our days, and since we are stuck in Erzurum for several consecutive days, they multiply and intensify, beginning with the relationship that we strike up with our hosts. The Turkish hospitality that we experience exceeds all of our expectations.

After having crossed their paths in a street where Milan was holding a diabolo show, Enes and Kadir, two young teachers, show us a memorable time. From a Middle-Eastern tinged dance-filled evening with endless cups of iced tea to a visit to the mosque and Milan's introduction to an ablution and prayer ceremony, Enes gives us the opportunity to live at the pace of his city.

Hikmet has heard of our trek from the Turkish media and stops us at the exit of the mosque to ask us to join him. Thanks to him, we meet his friends and colleagues Yayuz, Dayut, as well as his nephew, Josep. They are all beautiful people who change the course of our journey. Dayut sets us up in one of the rooms of his hotel, the Grand Erzurum, and assures us that we can stay there for as long as we need to. This is a charming gesture, that shows a rare generosity, and yet makes us feel uncomfortable... it is easy to cross the line between accepting a kind gesture and taking advantage of someone else.

We spend many moments with Josep. Our bond grows larger every day with this young man from Barcelona who speaks impeccable French. He joins us and is present during an astounding encounter with Christelle and Thomas, a traveling couple from Alsace who, for the last five months, have roamed the roads of Europe, and now Asia, on bike.

Forgetting about the kilometers that we must travel across, we adapt to the slow pace that has been imposed on us. Without losing sight of our objective, we let ourselves go with the flow of our encounters and the personalities we meet. We take advantage of the places we see, and we discover the surrounding areas of the city. We create new points of reference, such as the El Molino café, which becomes our shelter, our command post. The staff there are adorable and receive us during each of our stops with black tea and cakes. When the morale falls to such a point, these little details count twice as much.

The exceptional hotel in which we are staying comforts us as well. Located in the outskirts of Erzurum, it is at the foot of the ski resorts of Palandöken and Konakli, which are situated at 3,180 meters of altitude. Here, we take an open-air hike with Josep and Dayut, and this helps clear our minds and spirits – definitely giving meaning to the expression "to rise above"! Nature surrounds us here, the dusty and winding paths leading us to the peaks, the wind blowing in our faces, sweeping away all negative thoughts and reinvigorating our minds.

After five days in Erzurum, we finally leave the rain and the cold, full of hope, to go to Trabzon, thanks to Hikmet who has financed our bus tickets. The city possibly holds the solution to our problems, since the IT systems of the Iranian consulate are working once more after breaking down, and the acquisition of a visa there seems to be quicker.

After getting off the bus, a maritime ambiance surrounds us. The air is gentle at the beginning of autumn, the streets are lively and the terraces full. The contrast with Erzurum is satisfying, and the friendliness is attractive. With high spirits, we take advantage of the occasion and enjoy, for an evening, this short stay in the region where my family comes from. During this time, we receive an even more beautiful surprise: we run into Dayut, a student, who serves us specialties from the Black Sea before hosting us in his home for the night.

From the moment we wake up the next day, we hasten to knock on the doors of the consulate. The wait is long, but Milan finally can explain to the authorities his case, which is studied carefully. The much-awaited visa can be given to us the next day at the end of the day. We almost jump for joy; almost, because we still have to wait. At the same time, we receive a call from the Iranian Embassy in Erzurum that announces to us that the authorization number delivered by the Ministry of Foreign Affairs has finally arrived and that the visa can be expedited. Without thinking twice, we look at the time and we calculate: it is midday. Five hours from here to Erzurum. If we're lucky, we can arrive just in time to obtain our precious treasure. Without a minute to lose, we head toward the bus station. The manager of the bus company, Tuncay, a gem, offers us the return tickets without batting an eye, and our impatience keeps us awake the entire way. Josep picks us up at the Erzurum station and drives us to the embassy. Alas, the door are shut; we didn't have the right schedule in our minds. We must push our departure for the next day, but Josep's company helps us quickly forget this bad fortune.

After eight whole days of waiting, we can finally obtain the visa. The authorities approve the document and Éric, our sponsor, has paid the procedures. Our excitement and joy have returned, and the relief is immense. Optimistic Traveler can now continue with its challenge, furthering the exploration and trying to reach the objective of eighty days, even though the path matters more than the schedule. The challenge has begun again, and with it, the ballet with the vehicles that help us, step by step, advance.

Yildirim and Aydin drive us by car to Ağri, and we reach the border of Turkey on board a delivery truck. A last stop in a restaurant allows us to meet an Iranian man who speaks perfect French. With the intent of facilitating our next steps, we ask him to write a presentation of our adventure in his native language.

Twenty-third day of the adventure. The metal gates of the border post appear at the end of the paved road. We leave our driver and walk the rest of the way. We pass by the doors and validate our entry into this new territory. We're on the other side, in Iran, finally.

An enormous joy fills us after five days of uncertainty. It is even bigger in the face of this country that we know nothing about.

We begin searching once more for vehicles to travel in. The driver of a bus empty of passengers accepts to let us climb aboard, and this way, we reach the small city of Tabriz. Night has fallen, and we are torn between finding a new vehicle to travel in and finding a place to stay for the night. Just a few steps down the street are enough to make us enjoy the warmth and the hospitality of the Iranian locals. Here, Ahtem offers us a meal. There, Hussein invites us to share some tea.

When Milan finds out that a bus is leaving for Tehran, we jump to the occasion. Ali, of Turkish origin, attempts to convince Aliriza, the driver, to allow us to get on. To our great surprise, the negotiation, which was more of a conversation, convinces Aliriza pretty quickly.

The hum of the motor rocks us to sleep. In the dark night, we ride peacefully toward Tehran.

22 DAYS = 5 247KM

TURKEY

Istanbul

Ankara

Göreme

Trabzon

Erzurum

Elazığ

Muş

Ahlat

IRAN

Gürbulak

TURKEY

Day 24 – Thursday, October 2nd, 2014
Tehran, Iran

The road to the Iranian capital is long. We haven't been able to sleep very well, even though the bus is surprising spacious, however we're relieved when we think about how our delay has been greatly diminished due to the 1,200 kilometers we've made up during this bus trip.

The sun has risen when we reach Tehran. The morning crowds at the bus station surprise us, but we're quickly faced with a new challenge: the language barrier. The ease we felt in our communications so far, thanks to Muammer's command of the Turkish language, is now very limited and, for the first time since our departure, it is very difficult to find people who speak English.

We manage nonetheless to get directions to the downtown area and tourist attractions thanks to a man who gives us a metro pass, which is recharged later by a high-school student. This allows us to find our way around the city. Tired and dazed from the long bus ride, the unknown, and the change of climate and environment, Muammer collapses from exhaustion on a public bench. Later, we decide to spend the day just visiting the city; relaxation and serenity are on the program for today.

This serenity isn't easy to achieve due to the less-than-enthusiastic reception we receive in the cafés and restaurants we visit, as well as the limited access to the internet and certain sites, like Facebook and YouTube. This isn't helpful to us but we soon learn that there are codes to allow for a connection. We struggle to find something to eat even though, at this time, we aren't yet too hungry.

The second difficulty we must face is definitely the cultural difference. The dress code, the cultural practices, and the rules of etiquette of the Iranian people are foreign to us, and we attempt to avoid offending the people we meet with our behavior. We also try to not fall victim to the panic brought about by the concerned warnings we received about this country, but it is hard to do. An unexpected ID check and a police-enforced ban on filming initially throw us off, but happily the occasional encounters we have during the day clear our minds and reassure us.

In our hunger to discover the city and, after a few discussions about where to go first, we decide to head to the Milad Tower, a telecommunications tower located in the International Trade and Convention Center of Tehran. Upon arriving, we are guided to Afsaneh, whose unmistakable French is like music to our ears. Thanks to the young woman, who convinces her manager and the security team, we gain access to the tower and our guide leads us to the summit. From this viewpoint, we realize just how immense the capital city is. The mountains mark the northern limits of the periphery while toward the south the horizon is lost in the haze. We take advantage of Afsaneh's presence to learn more about the cultural aspects that intrigue us. We talk about several subjects, at first light, such as learning French in Bordeaux, and then heavier ones such as the wearing of a headscarf.

"I want to be able to express myself in whatever way I please, to wear what I want; to be free," she tells us in an assured manner. We can't help but to smile and to agree in the face of such determination.

We continue our quest and, later in the evening, we are led by a young man to a CouchSurfing get-together that is happening in the amphitheater of a park. Fate truly likes to pay tricks on us! The small group invites us to take part in the discussions and our adventure is fascinating to the people gathered. Bilal, of Pakistani origins, teaches us about his country and gives us the contact information of people he knows in Lahore. He also translates into Urdu a written summary of our challenge so that we can easily communicate once we arrive in his country - what luck! We also talk about the sociocultural evolution that is taking place in Iran, and we learn that the younger generations are leaning toward a greater freedom of expression, changing the preconceptions of the relationships between men and women, and reasserting their right to be able to choose their studies and to travel.

This exchange enriches our knowledge of the country and feeds our souls: the essence of our journey is here, right in front of us.

We continue our day's journey in the company of Leïli who, without thinking twice, invites us to stay the night at her place. Her invitation shatters another stereotype about women that we had been warned about; how many times have we heard the common warning "Don't talk to women and don't look them in the eyes, it's dangerous!"? However, we still feel apprehensive. Are women allowed to host men by themselves? What would the fathers or brothers think when they see us? We set these worries aside in the spirit of not creating problems for her and we enjoy a lovely evening together. Seated on rugs and cushions on the floor of her brother's apartment, we meet the young woman's mother, and upon Leïli's insistence, we wash our clothes and wear her father's outfits - long pants called "shalvar" and a shirt - when she offers them. Afterwards, we share a meal while talking about the many subjects that are dear to her. Her curiosity is refreshing, and her enthusiasm is contagious.

"My life in Iran is satisfying, but I constantly feel the need to see new things, otherwise ennui sets in."

This is a wise point of view that we approve of, and that we try to keep in mind day by day.

Day 25 – Friday, October 3rd, 2014
Tehran – Isfahan, Iran

It is with this same thought in mind that we begin our new day on Iranian soil. We gather our clean and dry clothes hanging on clotheslines spread out on the already sunny terrace. We take advantage of a hose to take a shower on the roof and we share breakfast with our hostess before setting out.

Leïli is both hesitant and enthusiastic with the idea of accompanying us all the way to Isfahan. At times confiding in us, at times reserved, she seems to be ceaselessly on guard. The situation is reversed many times and not always in a way that we understand, so we're occasionally confused. We feel powerless when witnessing a disagreement between Leïli and the driver of a taxi we catch. The tone rises between the two but, since we can't understand a single word of their dispute, we can't intervene, and the young woman suddenly closes up. We separate on this negative note before reuniting at the bus station at the beginning of the afternoon.

Here, the tensions dissipate after a diabolo show from Milan attracts the attention of the employees and customers of a bus company and, after a long wait, we manage to obtain two tickets to Isfahan. Once on board, Leïli, moved by what she's just witnessed, can't stop thinking about the generous gesture and she confesses that this demonstration of kindness has changed her point of view and has broadened her perspectives.

We reach Isfahan at sunset. We are grateful for Leïli's guidance in this city that she knows well. She takes us straight to the Imām Square and we are marveled upon the discovery of the Shah Mosque and its multicolored ceramic details, its sumptuous palaces, the majestic arches, and the bewitching shops of the Great Bazaar. The Middle-Eastern magic is enchanting, and the Iranian crafts charm us. Fascinated, we observe with interest the ancestral technique of printing on fabric with engraved wooden blocks, then we navigate the alleys and hungrily take in the antiques, the Persian rugs, the jewelry, and the lamps that shine brightly.

Our wanderings lead us to a restaurant in the heart of the old city. There, we are flabbergasted when we meet a magnetic personality: dressed completely in white, all the way to the tip of his long beard, Kalender is intriguing. Thanks to the two young women who accompany him and to Leïli, who translates, we manage to strike up a conversation. A Sufi in the Order of the Whirling Dervishes[6], he is avowed to his mystical cult that requires vows of poverty and austerity, and which privileges the essence of humanity before any religious or nationalistic affiliation.

Invited to his table by the owner of the restaurant, we continue to learn more before Kalender proposes that we stay at his home for the night, and this is an offer than we cannot refuse. The evening continues, and even more people expand our group. We are joined by many individuals, notably Payan, the owner of the neighboring restaurant, who surprises us by speaking in French. We leave the establishment and we pass

---

6   'Sufism' is a spiritual movement which began in the early 8th
     century. It is characterized by particular values, ritual practices,
     doctrines and institutions and represents the main manifestation
     of mystical practic in Islam. The whirling dervishes are members
     of the Mevlevi order.

again by the square. Small groups of people scattered on the grass share candies and tea, and the friendliness and human warmth are beautiful to see.

Respect and tolerance are present everywhere. Milan soon launches into a performance of diabolo as a way to thank our hosts, and attracts quite a crowd. Kalender is also attracted by the show, but doesn't take long to set off on his way, and we quickly follow him through the streets until we reach his apartment.

Inside there is one room, a recessed bed, some books and photographs, rugs, and cushions. We sit in a circle around Kalender, who captivates his audience with his poems and his speeches. Payan and Leïli attempt to translate what the Sufi is saying, and even though we can't completely understand everything, we easily capture the energies and vibrations we feel.

The moment is strong and memorable. Our message of humanity, 'to show the world that there are good people everywhere, in every country, religion, of every color and social category', is completely relevant here in Iran. Tonight, this helps us to happily accept the difficulties we have lived so far and to look ahead to the ones to come with a lighter spirit.

Day 26 – Saturday, October 4th, 2014
Isfahan – Yazd, Iran

We wake up in the dwelling of the Sufi, well-rested and with a great feeling of safety. Payan picks us up, as we had agreed upon last night, and we dedicate the morning to visiting the old city in a more in-depth way in Payan and Leïli's company.

Isfahan is a captivating place. No matter if it is at night or during the day, the city reveals its beautiful finery and culture. The architecture has a strong Islamic influence and these artisanal creations, with influences from both the Middle-East and Asia, marvel us. The engravings found throughout the city are full of religious symbolism, the stone walls of the Shah Mosque fill us with their divine presence and their ancestral energy, and the gardens and fountains keep the peace and the calm. These places have a thousand stories to tell.

While we walk in the streets, the small shops ensconced under the arches reveal to us many treasures. Repeated hammer strikes fashion copper and tin plates and cauldrons and mark the beat of our steps, while the aromas of spices stimulate our senses. We let ourselves be carried away by our discoveries and we pray that the exploration will never end...

Unfortunately, our departure time is drawing near. Leïli and Payan accompany us to the bus station and act as our intermediaries with the manager of the bus company in order to procure two tickets on the next bus to Yazd. We regretfully leave Isfahan and our new friends behind, but the excitement of the adventure still ahead doesn't take long to make us want to keep moving forward.

The bus has barely begun moving before we strike up a conversation with our neighbors, Safora and Sima. Once again, the stereotypes concerning the place of Iranian women in society are crushed in just a few words.

"The images of Iran that are spread out around the world are false," explains Sima. "They date from the generation of our grandparents and even before. Our parents were already growing up with a new mindset. Education and an open-mindedness to the world change many things."

Even though she is reserved and polite, the young woman isn't afraid to share her convictions and beliefs with two strangers, two men on top of that. Opening up her world to two tourists is a much better way to spend her time than to let herself be influenced by unfounded fears, she confesses. On that, a simple phone call to her parents to ask for permission and the deal is settled: we have a place to stay for the night. This is a godsend, since sleeping in the home of locals is assuredly what we prefer in this challenge.

We arrive in Yazd when night has fallen. Our evident joy delights Sima, who is obviously not accustomed to this type of public demonstration. Shahram, her cousin, greets us at the station with his wife Zahra and his four-month-old daughter, Shyli. We first stop to drop off the women – Sima, following a common ritual, is participating tonight in a gathering between all the women in her and her suitor's family – before Shahram takes upon the role of tour guide and leads us in the discovery of his city.

Taking his mission to heart, he explains to us the ancient history of the city, and shows us the underground irrigation systems and the aeration and natural climate control chimneys spread out through Yazd. We follow him through the tunnels and the streets of the old city until we reach an ordinary-looking door. Imagine our surprise when we discover that behind it and along a long corridor is a splendid historical dwelling that serves as both a tea salon and a hotel. The immense main hall is decorated with beautiful gilded woodwork. Seated on magnificent Persian rugs, we sample delicious pastries accompanied by a steaming tea; a wonderful moment.

We climb into the car again and pick up Zahra and Shyli before going back to their home. Once inside, we are taken aback by their attention to us. We set up for dinner on a cloth on the floor, and we help out in the kitchen, enjoying afterwards a succulent dinner with traditional Iranian accents. Saffron rice and dried raisins, chicken with yogurt, salad, and fruits; our taste buds are wholeheartedly enjoying this feast. Even more than the delicious meal, we savor our good fortune at finding ourselves tonight in the company of this family, something of uncountable value in our, and our hosts', minds.

Day 27 – Sunday, October 5th, 2014
Yazd – Kerman, Iran

The sun rises, and we are still in the family's home. The young Shyli gurgles as we eat our breakfast, and Zahra gets ready for her day. We all leave together to visit the ancient city of Yazd underneath a bright sun. We visit the mosque and its minarets, the highest in the whole country, and the bazaar and its little shops, where artisans and shopkeepers are buzzing with activity. We pass by a renovated hammam, a prison, and a school, all the while listening to Shahram, who takes us to every nook and cranny in the city and tells us anecdotes, such as the one concerning these wooden doors equipped with two door-knockers: the distinctive sound of each, he says, allowed the person inside to know who was knocking, a man or a woman. We taste culinary specialties and experience moments that often provoke fluttering inside us. Our European taste buds are disquieted by this bowl of soup with noodles and small balls that look suspiciously like fish eyes... what will we do if we don't like it? Can we refuse to eat something without offending our friends? These questions fill our minds; we are certainly at the heart of our cultural differences.

The time has come to honor an invitation to celebrate, at Sima's father's house, one of the most important festivities in the Muslim religion, Kurban Bayramı[7]. The entire family has gathered and greets us warmly. The structure of the house, similar to all the other Iranian houses, is organized around a large hall that acts as the main room. Upon first glance, it seems like all the men and women are separated into two groups, but we soon understand that this is more out of force of habit and preferences rather than a strictly established rule.

The conversations flow freely, and laughter rings out throughout the room. One of my diabolo performances captivates the room, generating a contagious enthusiasm, and the festivities are well underway. The music enchants the children and the men and leads them to perform frenzied dances. The women, amused and moved by the show, encourage them and clap to the rhythm.

We are delighted by the grandmother's hysterical laughter, deeply touched by the notes of the traditional chants, and succumb to the delicacies of Iranian cuisine. We can't get over the joy that has been given to us today in this incredible experience. Here, sharing our common values, we can see that humanity is at its zenith.

We feel even more touched when Sima's father comes toward us presenting gifts: a box of candies and two hand-painted eggs made by Sima herself, symbols of a new life and happiness. Sima later whispers to us that it is thanks to us that the day has been this joyful, and we are delighted to hear this moving confidence.

Full of memories, of smiles and kind looks, of phone numbers and e-mail addresses, we depart to the bus station with Shahram and his uncle. We look at the schedules and decide

---

7   'Kurban Bayrami', called the 'Sacrifice Feast' is one of the
     holiest Muslim holidays.

to attempt hitchhiking in order to leave sooner. Still accompanied by our hosts, we stop on the edge of the highway, in the darkness of the night, to find a vehicle to ride in. Here, we witness an incredible scene: Shahram, his uncle, and the policemen that have stopped by, all take it upon themselves to stop all of the trucks and cars that advance toward them. Unfortunately, the search is fruitless. We head to the bus station once more, where in a show of continued generosity, Shahram buys us the tickets we need.

The departure to Kerman is at 11 PM. We follow our friends to their car and thank them effusively. After, to distract himself during the wait, Muammer decides to practice with the diabolo. We take advantage of the moment to remember how we've spent this magnificent day, and then, suddenly, we see Yen and two of his friends arrive at the station. We had met him at the Iranian Embassy in Erzurum and we see him again here, in Yazd, more than 2000 kilometers away. What an unexpected surprise!

This is the magic of our journey.

Day 28 – Monday, October 6th, 2014
Kerman – Zahedan, Iran

We get off the bus at the Kerman bus station at 4 in the morning. We are exhausted. Today we are in transit, with our objective being the city of Zahedan, our last stage in Iran before reaching the Pakistani border. This type of travel helps us advance many kilometers, but the fatigue makes us feel like we are not connecting to the people and this isn't helping our already delicate exchanges.

As soon as we arrive, we attract curiosity from the people at the station. Even though it is early in the morning, the crowds already gathered there are impressive. Groups of laborers sleep on the benches, while others look at us with their faces covered in black fabric. Their local dress make us feel conscious of what we're wearing; we realize that we won't be unnoticed in the landscape of this region, and that it would be prudent to dress appropriately during the rest of our journey.

Obtaining tickets to Zahedan is a real saga: back-and-forth conversations, refusals, sudden changes of situation, suspense, and unexpected outcomes... we live a little bit of everything. Even though we have obvious trouble communicating, it seems to us that the manager of the bus company doesn't have the best relationship with his drivers.

We nonetheless manage to get on the bus. Milan, who in the meantime has managed to catch the sympathy of some young workers, gets on with a huge smile on his face because he is carrying in his hands a Baloch costume, used but complete, that one of the young men has generously given to him in exchange for our box of Iranian candies.

We set off on a nine-hour-long trip. The bus is jam-packed and noisy, and we slide into a spot made for us by a small group who squeezes together as much as possible, a gesture that surprises and touches us. We also share a few words in English with the young Mohammed and, after a small pause, with Abdulhamid, who offers us something to eat. After we get off the bus, the heat is overwhelming; we can now forget the breezy temperatures of the late summers that we're used to. Here the desert surrounds us, the sun beats down on our backs, and the shade is rare.

When we finally reach Zahedan, Abdulhamid offers to drive us to the English language school so that we can find help more easily. There, we are immediately received and we find ourselves at the front of a class, presenting and briefly explaining our adventure. We don't have to wait long for a response, as Amin, the teacher, invites us to spend the night at his home. We wait until the end of his classes and then follow him to his place. We meet his mother, and then his brother, Reza. We converse with the two young men about traveling and the future around a meal in a restaurant in the center of the city, and then we go back to their home to look over the rest of our itinerary with them. We spend a lovely evening in their good company.

We consider us to be rather lucky tonight, and are surprised in the face of this reception, of the hospitality, and of the selflessness of our new hosts.

Day 29 – Tuesday, October 7th, 2014
Zahedan, Iran

For the first time during the challenge, we dedicate an entire day to the preparation of the next stage. We are approaching Pakistan, and the extremely unstable climate in that country and its border zones won't leave any space for errors. We received many warnings concerning our safety but we nonetheless feel persuaded that, with good recommendations and with an adequate behavior, this crossing won't be impossible.

Thus, we spend the whole day accompanied by Reza and Amin, gathering all of the advice and opinions that we find judicious from bus companies, school teachers from the English language school, or from locals. Alex, a friend of Amin's, shares with us what Chris, a Belgian traveler, has recently experienced. According to him, the train line no longer works, but it is possible to find a bus, even without money. His status as a tourist is also very useful to us because he tells us to avoid filming or taking photos, especially when in the middle of crowds, and he confirms what we had thought before: that a local costume is definitely recommended.

In order to find one, we head in the direction of the Baloch market, on the other side of the city. We skim the shops and accumulate the refusals of the shopkeepers until Nader finds us and tells us that he can give us one of his costumes. With both of us now dressed in sarouel pants and tunics, we go home and put the last touches on our preparations: we cover our conspicuous backpacks with a sheet of white fabric. We are finally ready to leave for Pakistan.

The apprehension in the face of danger and uncertainty looming over the next days don't faze us. We rest optimistic, but not unconscious of them. "They are all terrorists!", "They're dangerous!", or even "You will be taken hostage!"... all of the remarks and warnings concerning our safety emitted by many people that we've crossed paths with before resonate in our minds, among our own, often unfounded, prejudices. For the first time during this challenge, we feel the need to reconnect with the people around us, and quickly. Their soothing and fraternal voices calm us down and give us the confidence we need to keep moving forward.

Our emotions are tested by the adventure and its tough challenges every day, and yet we discover a little bit more about ourselves every step of the way in this exploration of the world.

Day 30 – Wednesday, October 8th, 2014
Zahedan – Meer Jawe, Iran

We set off at the break of dawn on this thirtieth day of the adventure, leaving Reza and Amin in a parking lot at the edge of the city. Given the number of trucks that pass by this point, we hope to be able to find a driver to get to the border as soon as possible, but this is a hope that slowly ebbs away as the hours go by.

The vehicles are unmoving and their drivers don't offer a single hint as to when they will depart, so we decide to try hitchhiking along the edge of the road. The wind is kicking up the dust, and the heat of day is starting to beat down on us. The truck that we believe is going to deliver us from this frustrating wait turns out to be the just the beginning of an endless day.

The truck is turned back on, advances a few meters, and then turns around. We drive for several minutes before we reach a checkpoint. In the beginning, we wonder if the driver wants to announce our presence to the authorities, but we soon realize that he wants to turn us in at the police station. Once I understand his intentions, I order him to stop, and luckily we get off next to a taxi station. Milan suggests that we still go to the police station in order to signal our operation and to be escorted by the police themselves, if possible, as we were advised to do by the two English professors in Zahedan. Milan is maybe not used to frequent police checks, whereas I always avoid this kind of action, due to a fear of facing corrupt agents. Milan, however, wins his case and we do as he suggests, however this first checkpoint is only the first of many.

As much as the procedures seem normal at first, it still takes us 12 hours to travel only 75 kilometers. It is a question of safety, we are assured by the policemen. The representatives of the Iranian State would rather escort us; the kidnapping of two Europeans would present a negative image of their country.

Twelve hours. Almost two dozen checks of our IDs and photographic equipment. Unending questions left and right. Armed escorts. Six vehicles. Fifty mobilized troops. All of this punctuated by misunderstandings brought about by the language barrier.

The wait, which sees us spending up to our hours in the same place, is hard to deal with. The stress and the anguish we feel are paired with the inactivity and uncertainty that have colored our day. The presence of weapons doesn't help to calm us down, but the calm and sympathetic looks that the often young soldiers give us are paradoxically reassuring. We feel hungry and thirsty, but we are not alone, as our military escorts have the same needs as we do. The sun is striking, and the dusty wind is irritating to our throats. We squeeze alongside the soldiers into the little bit of shade that a wall provides. Sitting on the ground on a thin mat, we pass around the only bottle of water that we have in our possession. This is a moment of sharing that soon turns into one of relaxation and of taking a few photos.

The desert landscape adds a dramatic and magnificent touch to this day. The sharp relief of the mountains cut the sky, and the sand and dust swirl all the way to the horizon. The environment we find ourselves in is certainly extraordinary.

Then, suddenly, the tone changes. A soldier leads us into a shack. A new inspection of our possessions leads him to an exceptional discovery: the small pouch that we have placed between our pants and our underwear that holds our identity papers. A precious hiding place that allows us to always carry

70

our passports with us. To lose them now would be simply unthinkable! Without a word, he examines the documents spread out in front of him, looks at us, again scrutinizes the papers, takes a photo of them, and then makes a phone call. His suspicion is disquieting. Our precious passports pass from hand to hand and we won't see them for the rest of day. He lets us out of the shack and we wait, stunned. An impeccably-dressed man soon appears. His severe demeanor, his civilian clothing, and his mastery of the English language put an idea in our heads: is he from the Secret Service? The heavy interrogation and the body searches we face seem to confirm our fears. We stay calm and follow our orders without protesting. Milan wishes to call our entourage in order to inform them of our situation, but I refuse: we are going through a difficult moment but we aren't in danger. I am more concerned about scaring our families and friends and making them feel anxious and panicked at their inability to help us out. Thus, I do my best to reassure him, and with time, everything thankfully ends well.

Our nervous fatigue reaches its peak when we reach the isolated village of Meer Jawe, still in Iran, mere kilometers from the border. Once we present, for the umpteenth time, the goals of our project and why we have no money, a policeman accepts to pay us a hotel room. Thanks to the letter in Farsi explaining our adventure I try to negotiate with the receptionist to get something to eat. Sensitive to our condition, he leads me to a general store, who graciously gives me a bottle of water, some cakes, and dried fruit.

Finally alone, we let out a sigh of relief as we realize what we just lived through. We feel vulnerable in the face of our limited freedom; we feel new perceptions that trouble us and make us think, each at his own pace. We reflect on the challenge that we have set for ourselves, on our reactions to the knocks we have received, and on the way that they have destabilized us.

But most of all, we think about the good fortune that we have in this precise moment to be together, to be two.

Day 31 – Thursday, October 9th, 2014
Meer Jawe, Iran – Dalbandin, Pakistan

Still shaken from the events of yesterday, we wake up at a good hour, hoping that we won't have to live another difficult and hellish day. We quickly eat some bread and dates, the only meal that we've had in the last thirty-six hours, before meeting with the policemen in the reception of the hotel and getting in their car.

We reach the border rather quickly, but once we go into the no-man's-land things get complicated. The policemen have doubts about our honesty and can't fully grasp the objectives of our project. The interrogations recommence, and the forms to fill line up in front of us... To feel sensations of guilt for a crime that never existed is overwhelmingly strange. Nonetheless, we manage to enter Pakistan and are driven to the adjacent military base, where we have to wait once more.

There, the ancient barracks are circled with fences and are in the middle of the desert. There is not a single blade of grass to be seen, and the landscape is comprised entirely of sand and rocks. The soldiers seem surprised to see us arrive in their austere universe. We observe their morning rituals of chant and prayer, and afterwards we tentatively strike up conversations with them. The atmosphere clears up once we show them some magic tricks and I take out my diabolo, but this moment is fleeting as a man comes looking for us and takes us to his office.

Once again: the wait. More papers to manage, more questions to answer, and always the same ones as before. After: nothing at all. Finally out of the watchful eye of the soldiers, we jump at the opportunity to launch our Plan B. We have learned that there is a bus that leaves in the afternoon. Following a small dirt path, we reach the nearby village of Taftan. The soldier in charge of watching over us soon notices our absence, and we can feel the agitation behind us. The adrenaline surges, especially since we have continued to document our experience with a hidden camera, but serenity is of the essence here and we try to remain calm.

We find shelter in a small bakery, but our escape does not last long. The civil police follow the traces to our location, but they surprisingly let us enjoy this pause and to drink tea and warm bread before taking us to the chief's office. Here, once more, we are surprised by the lack of uniforms. Are these people truly policemen? The situation clears up a little because we are able to talk to an intermediary in English, but money, or our distinct lack of it, definitely poses a problem. We need to find a compromise because we cannot pay the taxi that he proposes to us and he cannot allow us to take the bus.

The solution eventually comes from his superior: the dice have been thrown, and we will be escorted by the police for 600 kilometers, all the way to Quetta.

The numerous checkpoints set the pace of our trip as well as the multiple change of vehicles, where we have a chance to stretch our legs. The straight road stretches infinitely ahead of us as the temperature climbs constantly throughout the day. Muammer attaches a scarf to his hat, and this combination is an ideal protection against the trio of sun, wind, and dust.

Looking at the horizon and armed to the teeth, our escorts are focused. Nevertheless, the atmosphere in the vehicle is far from heavy, and the looks they give us are full of understanding. We aren't the only people accompanying the soldiers today: Ilker, of Turkish origins, is traveling with us. His smile and his relaxed appearance are like antidotes to our apprehensions. His company is a true gift to us in these moments.

When we arrive in Dalbandin, we follow Ilker directly to a hotel where he invites us to share his room. A policeman will stay to keep an eye on us the entire night since we are forbidden to leave the building. From the balcony, we can see the streets and the establishments of the locals. Clouds of dust accompany each movement of the cars driving by and dissipate in the landscape made up of basic brick and dirt constructions. As night falls over the city, we are surprised by an apparition that emerges from the silent dark. A young boy of about 12 comes to find us, and his perfect English, his sweet and caring disposition, his knowledge, and his ambitions counterbalance the rough experiences we have had today. We receive a true message of hope and humanity in such a young person.

Relieved to see the day is over, we happily share a meal with Ilker. It is our first after forty-eight hours, and we appreciate every bite of potato, meat, sauce, and naan. We go to bed soon after with full stomachs and calm minds.

Day 32 – Friday, October 10th, 2014
Dalbandin – Quetta, Pakistan

It is now our second day in Pakistan, and the road is long to Quetta, the capital of the Balochistan Province. We are still in a dangerous area, due to our proximity to Afghanistan, so we must once again travel with a military escort, who has taken our passports again. The possibility to travel alone is non-existent since the train line is no longer in service and the buses don't accept tourists. After the dissipation of last night's tensions, the Pakistani police accept to take care of us today, and we are meeting at 8 AM. Ilker has just enough time to buy three bottles of water, and then we depart on a 300-kilometer-long journey across the desert landscape.

First escort, first car: the ballet begins once more. Surrounded by armed men and not understanding anything but the most basic of words in their language, we are taken over by a wave of apprehension. About 100 kilometers after, we get on a second car, and then a third. We learn that the escort zones are specifically marked, and the mobilized militia must take turns in transporting us in order to assure our safety.

The atmosphere of our trip is a heavy one. The cadence of our travel is deafening, marked by the throbbing of the loud motors and exhausting jolts. The sun is blinding and the wind, carrying thousands of grains of sand, whips our faces and dries our throats. The winding and chaotic roads seem endless on the back of the pick-up trucks we're riding, and we feel tired and hungry.

And yet, our feelings of unease ebb away with each kilometer we travel. Odd situations replace the instances of doubt, and we allow ourselves to relax and be pleasantly surprised by the light moments that we spend. Breaking for tea along the mountains in the middle of nowhere, surrounded by the police and truck drivers transporting gasoline, themselves also escorted... this is one of those moments. Another is when we find ourselves in the cab of the truck, the three of us squeezed into two seats, backpacks on our knees in this unbearable heat, and seeing that our only escort is a moped that clears our path...

The contrasts are endless.

We find a much more serious environment when we arrive in Quetta at night. The traffic increases, the trucks shudder with each stop, and the car horns ring out sporadically. Our vehicle slows down, and eventually stops. The driver cuts the gas, and slams the doors. Darkness and silence surround us.

After a discussion that sounded very delicate to our ears, we transfer to another vehicle and live our first experience traveling in an armored car, surrounded by an antiterrorist commando unit. Our stress increases and we ask many questions, but the journey continues, punctuated by the familiar changes of vehicles and followed by a disquieting blare of sirens. Two days earlier, a bomb was set off in the city's mosque. A week before that, there was a terrorist attack at the airport. We aren't doing anything but traveling across the country, but we are still witnessing the hardships lived by the people of this nation.

It has been a journey full of emotions and memories: the kilometers in the sand, the rhythm set by the police escorts, the chilling weapons. Twenty-three vehicles and more than one hundred police officers have been mobilized for this trip. We have spent twelve hours without eating a single morsel.

It has been an intense day, marked by our encounters, the faces, the looks, and the smiles of the people we've met, and also by the kindness and the human warmth that we've experienced, even in this disheartening context. And finally, by the reassuring presence of Ilker, who offers us a meal and a night in a hotel once we arrive.

This has been an incredible new stage of our journey, during which we've lived unprecedented experiences. And adventure? Always.

Day 33 – Saturday, October 11th, 2014
Quetta – Lahore, Pakistan

The calming, green environment of our hotel lulls us into a sense of well-being and tranquility after these last three days of traveling with a police escort. We take advantage of the moment to eat breakfast with Ilker in the garden and to study the plan of action for the day.

It is out of the question to once again submit to the authority of the army and push back our departure from Quetta until they allow us to leave. We have our passports in our pockets, so nothing stops us from sneaking out of the hotel and heading to the train station on a car that drops us off without losing a single moment. Ilker buys the tickets and once we're on the train all three of us feel a huge feeling of relief.

Finally, freedom! We have taken back the reins of our adventure.

The whistle marks our departure toward Lahore, and the trip is going to be twenty-six hours long. The train is packed, and we don't have assigned seats, so some passengers make some space next to them in their crammed compartment. This is a similar gesture to the one that we witnessed on the bus to Zahedan. Some of the locals, like Saif, speak English, and we are thrilled to be able to communicate with each other, especially about the cultural differences we have lived.

At each stop, waves of passengers crash into each other, getting on and off the train. During one of our layovers, Hasan signals to us to follow him and his friends, who are seated on the platform floor, ready to eat lunch. In the middle of the moving crowd, we enjoy the traditional cuisine that they share with us, and savor the unique moment that we are living.

We pass the time by spending hours observing our new environment: the Pakistanis and their piercing gazes, their serene attitudes, and their attractive smiles. We watch and we learn.

The sunset paints the sand dunes around us in shades of gold and orange. We soon leave the arid steppe of the Balochistan region, all while committing to memory the moments we've spent during this epic crossing. For the first time, without a doubt due to what we've experienced, the feeling of safety leads us to fall asleep at the same time. No more surveillance, and less fears: letting go of all that is a wonderful feeling.

Day 34 – Sunday, October 12th, 2014
Lahore, Pakistan

In the wee hours of the morning, we can see the fatigue on the passengers' faces. Some of them, like Ilker, have slept on the floor among the dust and the dirtiness, while others, ourselves included, have taken turns sleeping curled up on the benches. Sheets are hung up here and there to assure a little bit of intimacy to the passengers. Every little space is taken up, and moving around in the halls of the cars is extremely limited.

Outside, the morning haze covers the farmlands. The green landscape is vastly different from the one that we've lived in the last few days. We are now in the Punjab Province, the main agricultural region of Pakistan. As we get closer to our destination, the distance between the villages and the cities that zoom past grows smaller, and the buildings, oftentimes ruined, are scattered throughout.

We finally reach Lahore with an almost six-hour delay. Getting off the train involves a monumental scramble, and we're launched into a new universe, one that is chaotic and unknown. It is here, on the platform, that our path diverges from Ilker's. We share an embrace, and a look that transmits the gratitude and respect that we have gained for him, after the difficulties faced, and the troubles lived these last three days. His presence has truly marked the Optimistic Traveler adventure.

Outside of the train station, a cacophony reigns over the environment. The surge of vehicles and pedestrians sucks us into its hellish rhythm. We once again run into linguistic difficulties while trying to communicate with the locals even though we have our magical letter written for us by Bilal in Tehran. Thankfully, we soon run into Kharim, who speaks English well. We strike up a conversation with him and, one thing leading to another, arrive at a small restaurant. A sociologist with conviction, Kharim tells us about his people, pacifist and progressive, while ordering us something refreshing to drink. He says that he hopes to see his country create alliances to fight against the inflation and poverty plaguing the population.

After these optimistic words, Kharim leads us to a hotel in the same neighborhood. The owner, after a slight misunderstanding about the payment of the room, accepts to lodge us for the night. Even if the level of comfort is rudimentary at best, and the cleanliness of the room is hardly acceptable, we are still deeply grateful to him for offering us a roof to sleep under.

In the afternoon, we go out to explore the neighborhood. By chance, we pass in front of a barber shop, and with a knowing look at each other, we enter the establishment. After some words shared with the barber, we find ourselves seated in the tall chairs, ready to have our beards trimmed. The old-fashioned furniture is uncomfortable, but the service is impeccable. Each movement from the barber's hands is precise even though the dim light flickers out after five minutes. A man fiddles with two cables on a sign outside and the problem seems to be solved, at least for the evening.

We continue to walk around, proud of our beautiful mustaches. We multiply our encounters, and we sample many of the different specialties that are offered to us at various street food stands: spicy samosas, freshly baked naan, pomegranates, and bananas. It doesn't matter what we sample, our taste buds are delighted with every bite.

One last surprise allows us to close our final stage in Pakistan in a beautiful way. All around us, the streets are full of music, and the liveliness of a large tent calls out to us. We peek behind the thick curtains, and see inside that the festivities of two weddings are in full swing. Luckily, a member of the organization team ushers us in, and the radiant atmosphere transports us to the heart of the Pakistani culture. The traditional dresses of the women shine brightly, and the mischievous looks of the children present are captivating. We mix in with the crowd, which accepts us without a second thought. One diabolo show later and we are now definitely part of the party! Sadly, the celebrations must be cut short due to the strict rules of the city: marriage or not, the music and the lights must be turned off a 10 o'clock sharp!

Just another magical and luminous experience that won't be soon forgotten.

FROM
IRAN
TO
PAKISTAN

34 DAYS = 9 837KM

Gürbulak

Teheran

IRAN

Isfahan   Yazd

Kerman   Zahedan   Taftan   Quetta   Lahore

Meerjawe   Dalbandin

PAKISTAN

Day 35 – Monday, October 13th, 2014
Lahore, Pakistan – New Delhi, India

Even though we have slept in very basic accommodations, we wake up well rested, and leave the hotel bright and early to get a head start on our day. The loud, omnipresent noise and the endless traffic turn our heads, but we continue on our paths.

We meet a group of young students and briefly tell them about our project. Milan does a short diabolo presentation, which earns us some bills which we refuse so as to not betray the spirit of our challenge. They give them instead to the driver of a motorcycle who was attracted by the gathering. We climb on board the multicolored cart, and our driver takes us in the direction of a bus stop that serves a line connected to the Indian border. All along the way, we marvel at the unending line of Pakistani trucks, the famous brightly colored vehicles, each more beautiful than the last.

Our anticipation reaches its peak when we approach the border post, but we realize something that dampens the excitement of the moment: the disappearance of our GoPro camera, the second one we've lost during this trip. We decide to keep going, vowing to take better care of our third and last camera.

A young Iranian woman invites us to join her in her taxi, a lucky occurrence since the cars passing by here can be counted on one hand. From there, we decide to head directly to New Delhi. The euphoria and the joy we feel from arriving in India quickly dissipate, though, in the face of the harsh reality. The low quality of life and the extreme poverty we witness move us, and also put us in a delicate position. Nonetheless, here as in every other place so far, we are guided by our lucky star to a Good Samaritan who buys us train tickets. Our three-hour long wait flies by in our delight at this good fortune.

The Amritsar hockey team travels with us for part of the journey. The environment is cheerful, and they amuse themselves by transforming us into Sikhs and putting us in turbans. We allow them to work their magic on us, happy to share such a moment. Across the carriage, we also observe, fascinated, a young Sadhu[8] who doesn't let go of a golden effigy of Krishna. His bright, saffron-yellow robe, his hypnotizing gaze, and his elegance give him an exceptional charisma.

Night has completely fallen as we arrive in New Delhi. On the platform, we continue a conversation that we began onboard the train with Surinda and her husband, who we met when we went into the First Class carriages to attract attention to our challenge. We try to obtain information about the city and about the places where we could possibly stay. Surinda reflects, hesitates, and then leads us through the hallways of the station until we reach the exit. There, we meet one of her friends and we leave together in a car. We have no idea where we're going.

A few moments later, we are astonished to discover a Sikh temple looming in front of our eyes. The immaculate white architecture and the gold-plated cupola of the Gurudwara Bangla Sahib capture all of the light in the dark. Inside, a group of men explain to us that we can indeed sleep inside this place of worship. One of them, Lucky, points us in the direction of the hall, and then gives us his phone number and tells us we can sleep in one of his hotels.

In the large common hall, more than fifty men are sleeping on the floor. The opportunity to sleep in this holy place is

---

8   religious ascetic mendicant who has renounced the worldly life
     and keenly follows a path of spiritual discipline.

tempting, but we enjoyed our meeting with Lucky and we want to get to know him a little better.

He is not surprised to receive our call, and hastens to pick us up and take us to a small family hotel. A busy entrepreneur with a large network, Lucky is a captivating personality. We immediately feel a bond with this young man who is unfailingly generous. He is in a hurry, so he lets us install ourselves in our room, but he doesn't leave without first saying that we can count on him during our stay in New Delhi.

The rendezvous is set, then.

Day 36 – Tuesday, October 14th, 2014
New Delhi, India

We wake up in New Delhi, the capital of India, between the walls of a small hotel room. Yet another country to add to the list of the 80 Days Challenge, and what a country! Neither of us can hide our excitement. We both carry many images of India in our heads, and we are ready to go and seek them out. Without wasting a single second, we get ready to explore the city. Today is a day to rest, and there are no kilometers to beat, so we leave our bags in the hotel room; a blessing that assures us a greater freedom of movement.

We have barely left the hotel when we feel an incredible sensation. The charmingly particular environment around us picks us up and carries us away in a fraction of a second. Colors, sounds, and aromas have our senses on high alert, jostled by so much new information.

The traffic is dense, and creates a loud, constant sonic background. The car horns mix with the humming of motors, the bells, and the alarms, all of which give way to the sounds of many conversations that are barely audible over this brouhaha.

Visually, it is an explosion of details. At first glance, chaos seems to spread out before our eyes. A rickshaw passes by, then a bus, and then a car. A tuk-tuk speeds by the right of this line, and a motorcycle by the left. Add in a pedestrian here, a cow – a sacred animal in India – thundering by there. We don't understand anything, we just watch, and soon the chaos is transformed into a sort of ballet, each millimeter of each step meticulous.

All around us, the shops, the buildings, and the shacks all succeed each other and pile up haphazardly. Sheet metal and concrete, canvas canopies, terraces spilling into the animated streets - all of this swaying architecture amazes and scrambles up our Western sensibilities.

The fabric, sari, pashmina, and jewelry shops are a parade of color. The luminous logos here and there are connected by endless, suspiciously placed electrical lines surrounded by signs to try and somehow mask their occurrence.

Mixed in with all this is the street food that arouses the senses. The scent of cooking, smoky vapors or heavy frying, distil a heady spice cocktail of a thousand flavors.

On top of this busy facet, New Delhi shows another side. The Lodi Gardens are a jewelry box of greenery in the capital city. There, the vegetation is abundant, and the wind gently rustles the branches and palms caressing the white flowers. Couples come here to find refuge from the noise of the city, other come here to be revitalized.

85

The numerous temples, mosques, and places of worship inherent to Indian culture are inviting and offer moments to listen to oneself. Whether one is a believer or not, the multiplicity of religions and the importance of faith inspire respect and tolerance.

The architecture of these places is fascinating to us – and we are especially astounded by the magnificent artistry of the Lotus Temple. Visiting these places leaves us with starry eyes and satisfies our hunger of discovery.

This sensation isn't dampened by our contact with the population of the city. Poverty is unavoidably here, as well as the incomprehensible caste system, but we forget it all in the face of the smiles, the looks, the curiosity, the welcoming spirit, and the extreme kindness of the Indian people.

Without the intervention of Lucky, our Sikh lucky-charm and Bollywood actor from Sundar, his driver, and his friend who have showed us around the city, and the many vendors, shopkeepers, and tourists that we have met along the way, such as this Israeli family, our day in New Delhi wouldn't have been as rich as it has been...

Day 37 – Wednesday, October 15th, 2014
New Delhi – Agra, India

Second morning in New Delhi. Reinvigorated by the night and inspired by our yesterday, we plunge once more into our exploration of the city with all the impatience and energy of two young children.

So many things to do today!

First, we meet with Lucky to hand over our treasure: the memory cards that contain all of the videos and photos that we've taken up until now. They're going to retrace their steps back to Strasbourg to be kept in a safe place, thanks to his intervention.

Next, we find something to eat. Breakfast is the most important meal of the day, or so they say, and even when we are traveling around the world without money in our pockets, we try not to break the rule. Most of all, we can't resist the opportunity to meet new people. Back at the restaurant that we discovered last night, we speak for a few moments with two young English people living in Hong Kong, one working in finance and the other in real estate, who are passing through India. We meet voyagers almost every day; Earth is a playground for all of us.

A final mission, at last. We recall the dream of Recep, our Turkish friend from Muş. While waiting for the opportunity to one day be able to visit India, he gave us a T-Shirt to wear upon our arrival in this land, a symbol that followed us during our travel here. His wish is now fulfilled and we happily send him the photographic proof!
Afterwards, we walk for a long time in the direction of the train station. Weaving through the traffic and overwhelmed by the heat, dust, and pollution, we experience all of the bad sides of a mega-city. This is a negative aspect that we quickly leave behind once we're on the train to Agra, thanks to two tickets that were graciously given to us by Sundar last night.

Here, we are once again caught by reality. Seated in the wrong car, we barely escape a 600-rupee fine, something which would not have been advantageous to our situation in the slightest! We take advantage of the first stop to jump onto the correct car, and into another dimension. The train is packed to say the least. Everyone has difficulty finding a spot, and bags and suitcases fill the halls since the overhead luggage racks serve as seats for the passengers. Communication is difficult but looks don't lie. Intrigued and curious, the children riding the train do not stop staring at us. We speak a couple words of English with a family, in an attempt to find a group of friends en route to see the Taj Mahal. The trip is a truly deep dive into the heart of Indian culture, but this isn't enough for us, as the heat is sweltering and we soon seek a cooler spot. We later find refuge and some refreshing wind on the platform between two cars. The wind blows through the openings and the heat becomes a little more manageable, while the rocky tracks and the fields of dense vegetation slowly stream by us.

Once we arrive at the Agra train station, we leave behind the singular environment on the train. We are famished, but soon helped out by the owner of a small but engaging restaurant made all the more attractive by the sight of its smoking noodles that give our energy a boost.

We are now recharged, motivated, and mere steps away from the Taj Mahal - it is out of the question to miss this jewel of a landmark.

We are dropped off quickly at the entrance of what looks like a park and our battle begins. From a checkout booth to a control post, with positive and negative responses, from local tourists to foreigners, we shuttle back and forth for a while. The excitement rises and then falls, and the final response crashes down upon us like a guillotine blade. The fortress will keep hold of its precious jewel and we will not be able to visit the mythical, symbolic, and majestic palace today.

With a last look over our shoulders, we leave and head in the direction of downtown Agra. While walking through the streets, we are sucked into a parade. We don't know if it's a marriage, a procession, or another type of festivity, but the music draws us in and makes us forget our disappointment in the blink of an eye. This is a magical, colorful, and animated moment during which India reminds us mischievously that it certainly does hold many treasures.

In a tourist spot such as this, travelers aren't hard to find. By consequence or by simple fact, the locals are timid when we approach them. The night seems like it will be long without a place to stay. The hunger and fatigue that we feel, along with the refusals that we face, create a negative mood that attacks our good spirits. Disagreements between us are rearing their ugly heads...

However, all we need is to push open the door of the Sidhartha hotel and to meet its manager, Chandra, to make our night go in a different direction. Possessing a huge generosity, this man shares and offers us all that he can while still respecting the responsibilities of his job. Thanks to him, we will sleep with a roof over our heads tonight, in a clean room equipped with a shower and Wi-Fi. What a treat!

The evening ends on the roof of a restaurant with the joyful company of Jana, a Czech tourist guide, her group of tourists, and a Brazilian couple: we are surrounded by a good crowd. Underneath the starry sky, luck smiles at us again and again.

Day 38 – Thursday, October 16th, 2014
Agra – Orchha, India

In the early hours of the morning, while we're still nestled on a terrace overlooking the city of Agra, the calm fills us. From here, the view of the Taj Mahal is prodigious. The haze tints the sky with light shades of pastel on the horizon, and undulates between the heavens and the earth. The splendorous architecture of the palace that we can see in the distance is at stark contrast to the often dilapidated houses at our feet. The bird songs slowly wake us up, echoes of music surround us, and we smile, amused, when see the monkeys that balance on the edges of the roofs around where we stand.

The sky clears and lets the first rays of sunlight pierce through the clouds. The light turns pink, and then reddens, and it is now time to once again try to conquer the Taj Mahal. Will it open its door for us today? We can do nothing but cross our fingers...

There is less traffic than last night, but it is still surprising to see how many people are out and about this early in the morning. We quickly run into an Australian tourist who, being charmed by her visit, decides to buy us a ticket with the cash that she has left. Finally, the door-opener!

How will we decide who is going to profit from this experience? We decide to go with the tried and tested method of flipping a coin. A passerby accepts to lend us a coin and to witness the match. The coin is launched into the air, and Muammer, the winner, quickly reverses the rules:

"I give my ticket to my friend Milan!"

The surprise and incomprehension must have been noticeable on my face before being replaced by joy when I realize that Muammer is giving up his place for me.

Marveled, I walk along the long hallways accompanied by the group of young people we met on the train yesterday. I soak up every little detail on the immaculate white of the mausoleum's walls, whose marble reveals to the curious onlookers its carvings, interlacing, and inscribed writings.

At the same time, Muammer crosses the Yamuna River and arrives on the other side, ready to face the unknown. This quest leads him to meet some of the locals and to visit a new temple.

Once we're reunited, we pass by the hotel before meeting with Jana, the guide. Onboard a rickshaw, we leave toward the train station, seduced by the idea of taking a train to Orchha with the Czech tourists. Once we're at the station, we need to find someone to finance our tickets. The negotiations are difficult but Jana saves us by buying our seats.

We have a little bit of time before us and the temptation is impossible to resist when I notice a group of musicians. I now have a musical backdrop for a diabolo show! The musicians, however, are not enchanted with the idea, and neither is the police that soon comes to shoo me away. I guess it will have to be another time! Anyway, our departure is nigh.

On board the train, we continue our observation of this foreign culture. Here, we see a perfectly clear example of the separation of castes that is ubiquitous in India. A car that is jam-packed with people, and plagued with overwhelming heat, precedes another that is almost empty and refreshed with air conditioning.

After a few hours, we reach the small village of Jhansi. We continue to Orchha, ten kilometers to the south, on a rickshaw that is very evidently on its last legs, and motorcycles loaded with at least three people pass us with ease. At our sides, children follow our tracks, running and playing with an old tire and a stick.

For once, we decide to take our time to discover the small city. We are surprised by the amount of people on the streets and, driven by our desire to explore, we quickly lose sight of each other. Second separation of the day.

From this moment onward, our experiences differ.

Following the aroma of racks of food, and hypnotized by the colors, Muammer finds himself in the middle of the main plaza:

"In the shade of a large tree, on colored mats, fifteen Hindus are seated on the ground. Armed with sitars and percussion instruments, and dressed in turbans and long tunics that cover their sarouel pants, they call out to me to come and enjoy some tea with them. Their long white beards contrast with the darkness of their skin, and their eyebrows add to their already piercing gazes. Their faces are marked with the heat, the sun, and life itself. Feeling like I'm looking at a living painting of the local culture, I enjoy this moment. These men have a magnificent presence; their wisdom is clear in their every movement. Even though conversation through words is difficult, gestures and looks are more than enough to communicate. The music, which I let myself be carried by, is also helping to break the ice. A crowd gathers while the musicians play and sing. Minutes and hours go by, and the group is still here as if in a trance. Regretfully, I must leave them in order to see what else the city holds for me. A young Indian man, a barber, proposes to take me to his shop. After a detour to a temple and to his house a little later, and as the sun sets giving place to the night, here I am, freshly shaven, ready to set off to look for Milan."

Several hours earlier, after many discussions with the shopkeepers and the locals, I followed a completely different path.

Riding on a motorcycle, I leave to visit a first temple in the company of some locals. No music or singing for me; rather, I spend a moment of contemplation, meditation, and of sharing with my guide. Later, while climbing on the roofs and going higher and higher, another idea about the local lifestyle forms in my head. The view is magnificent and photogenic. Here, strong memories are branded into my mind.

Losing each other in this small city has allowed us live experiences that are simultaneously different from and parallel to each other, for the first time in this adventure. The richness of our human interactions here, our motor, fills us with happiness. Together or individually, we are able to find what we're seeking. The exchanges and the moments that we share with others help us continue with our trek. Nonetheless, we are convinced when we reunite later that night in the streets of Orchha, that to reach the end of this challenge, the adventure must be written by four hands.

Day 39 – Friday, October 17th, 2014
Orchha – Mahoba – Varanasi[9], India

Bothered by the mosquitos and other insects flying around, we couldn't have slept more than we have in our hotel room reserved for employees. The level of cleanliness is sometimes at the bare minimum, and outside, the well-tended gardens and oleander shrubs play a losing game of hiding the trash and filth on the ground.

This, however, doesn't stop us for a second. Happy to find ourselves in a small city, we abandon our makeshift shelter to go into the colorful and animated streets. We quickly run

---

9   'Varanasi' also known as 'Benares'

into an Indian man that Milan had met last night and have breakfast with him, where we enjoy, once more, the traditional street food: fried vegetable balls and a sweet dessert. We are certainly supplied with a high quantity of fats and sugars to replenish our energy!

We head to one of the numerous temples for a health walk. Impressed by the thick crowd milling around, we let ourselves be guided by our encounters. Once I am marked with a tilaka[10] on my forehead, we set off climbing the spiral staircases. Soon enough, the light all but fades, and we arrive at the top of the monument. Milan is delighted and rapidly scales the last steps which lead to a dome that looms above our heads. Below us, the people buzz around and there is loud music playing. We thank our guides for this unforgettable moment and we take our leave; the road is calling to us once again

Our goal today is to reach Mahoba by hitchhiking, and then continue on to the city of Varanasi. Turkey seems far away now, and we are happy to be able to recommence our favorite way of traveling. Now that we are out of Western territory, though, we have to change our tactics. People crowd around on the sides of the roads and cars aren't easily accessible from there, so we're going to need to jostle for a position where we're noticeable.

We manage to find a cooperative driver who already has six people in his vehicle. Evidently, the quantity of people doesn't faze them, and we soon find ourselves in the car, one in the trunk and one on the very edge of a seat, ready for a rather strange trip. We let ourselves be driven merrily along the road, listening to the notes of traditional music that fade away as the smoke from a conical pipe that's being passed around spreads

---

10   'Tikala' or 'Tika' is a mark worn usually on the forehead by a
      large number of Hindu people. It represents either a religious, a
      marital or a yoga-related signification.

out to every corner of the car... with bright eyes and blissful smiles, our travel companions are all soaring in the clouds. We don't think that simple tobacco can cause that sort of effect...

We are relieved when we pause for a while in the fresh air. A few odd encounters and a tea later, we set off again, albeit on a slightly different route than we had intended. We're dropped off in a small village where no one speaks a word of English, and we lose valuable time trying to explain our project and finding our way. Nonetheless, we manage to catch a bus that takes us to the road heading to Mahoba.

From that moment on, seated in the dark bus, the events of our day seem to be less chaotic. When we're dropped off, a car soon stops at our side. Its driver, Aashishh Kumar, and his friend both work in education, and we ride with them to Chhatarpur. They invite us to eat a meal in a restaurant that is eerily similar to one of the ones we would eat in back in Europe, and then they supply us with plenty of water and bananas before sending us off on a bus.

Finally, we reach Mahoba. There, we accompany Dirpal Singh Rajput, whom we met on the ride, to his home, but only after he has taken a look at our passports. We are a bit taken aback at this procedure, but thankful nonetheless. Reinvigorated after a nice shower, we share some tea with Dirpal, who tells us about his most beautiful story, his marriage, with his photo album there to provide a visual. We dive into his intimate story and his culture, in the heart of India with its bright local colors. We all leave together afterwards to catch a rickshaw heading to the train station.

The next train to Varanasi doesn't leave until 30 past midnight, so we have the whole evening before us. This is a good thing, since we still have to obtain tickets to ride the train. Intrigued by our adventure, a shopkeeper by the name of Shiran promises to help us out. He offers us a dish of vegetables, some water, and he drives us to his office, telling us to wait for him while he looks for someone who can help out. The satisfaction at calmly waiting for this man who has taken care of us is soon replaced by a feeling of impatience and doubt as the hours go by. Will he be back in time? Will he be able to buy us tickets?

Faced with growing stress, we react differently to the situation, and this elevates the tension between us. Milan cannot stay still, and he returns to the train station. He comes back a little while later with a ticket; a diabolo show has allowed him to collect enough money. Our principles are thrown into question by this action, and our opinions diverge. Our tones remain calm, though. We'll hold a second show to get a second ticket, and we'll have enough time to talk about this later. The departure time draws near, and we jump onto the train.

There are still no numbered seats, and there are more passengers than seats. We spend the night taking turns sleeping or at least resting for a bit on the overhead luggage racks or on the edge of a seat shared with a handful of passengers. This is a difficult night, but it is full of memories (and quite a few muscle cramps!)

Day 40 – Saturday, October 18th, 2014
Varanasi, India

We reach Varanasi on the night train. Exhausted by our journey, we must still walk hundreds of meters along the train tracks, next to the whistling trains, until we reach the platform. As we're launched into the city, we're stunned. It is swelteringly hot here, there are huge throngs of people around the train station, and the noise is incessant. Car horns, traffic, the crowds... everything seems to be aggressive at the moment. We are thrown off by all this and we feel lost, as if dealing with a significant amount of jetlag.

The adventure, however, goes off without a hitch, similarly to the way it went as we left Mahoba, except that we had been able to get some sleep there...

Our arrival in Varanasi, a sacred Hindu city, marks the mid-point of our adventure. We have been on the road for forty days, and forty more are still to come. We re nourished by our exchanges, we deal with the heavy blows, we accept the consequences, we get used to the differences, and then we leave, more motivated than ever to complete our challenge.

Seated in the back of a tuk-tuk, we let ourselves be carried away by the striking flow of the traffic. Penniless in the face of this circus, we cannot help our driver, who is having difficulties getting us anywhere, and we feel powerless. We decide to walk for a while in the mess of crowded streets.

Hugging the banks of the Ganges River, the old city, labyrinth-esque, unfolds before our eyes. As we make our way around the food stands and artisanal booths, we magically happen to come about the person who will become our spiritual and tourist guide for this day.

Debasish is not a simple silk and sari merchant. Adept in the skills of reiki[11], more specifically the neo reiki branch that he teaches, he shares with us, in a simple manner, his life philosophy and his point of view on Indian spirituality and energies. With a touch of humor, he illustrates the faith and the beliefs

---

11   'Reiki' is a form of alternative medicine originated in Japan
      which uses a technique called 'hands-on healing' through
      universal energy.

that his people hold.

"You, Westerners and Europeans, have these marks and wrinkles on your foreheads. Us, we don't blink unless God wants us to. We accept our Destiny, and this makes us free."

Truly calmed by this amazing discussion, we attentively listen to him. Later, he gives us hints to allow us to understand Varanasi. The Holy City doesn't leave us feeling indifferent – on the contrary, we're left wondering if our initial malaise in this city came from its indescribable nature. Varanasi cannot be described in a few words, one must cross it, go past the superficial in order to discover its true nature.

"More than that," he adds, "you must be worthy of what the city offers and possess something of value to share in return. In every way, Shiva is the guardian of this city. If he does not allow it, if he doesn't give you a free pass through the city, then you cannot be here."

On these words, we leave without waiting a single more second to explore the riches of the old city. We soon run into Cyril and Itay, Swiss and Israeli respectively, our two new companions. From the sun at its zenith to the fresh night air, we explore the narrow alleys, the food stands, and the ghats that lead to the Ganges River, where meditation and contemplation séances, religious ceremonies, and cremations are taking place. Slowly but surely, Varanasi reveals to us its secrets and its mysteries.

Animated by the soul of the city, and encouraged by Debasish's words, we have but one desire: giving back. Through juggling, music, and percussion, we throw ourselves into performing. Either by fascination or curiosity, small groups gather around us and the crowd thickens; we have succeeded in giving back to the city some of the magic that she has revealed to us. At least for a short moment, considering generosity is always surprising when it arrives. We thought that we would be the ones giving tonight, but we are also going to receive even more, and discover, stunned, that we have collected enough money to reach our next goal, Calcutta.

It is with joyful hearts that we follow Itay, our acolyte, to one of his friend's house for the evening. Sitting around a pot of tea, rocked by the music, we share rich discussions with Sara and Emilia, from Spain and Argentina. Even though our ways of thinking are different, we come together to talk about our life philosophies and our experiences. Each person is nourished from the spirituality of the next, as if new worlds were opening up to us at the very moment. The idea of bathing in the Ganges, a sacred river recognized as the most polluted in the world, comes about slowly. The rendezvous is set for tomorrow, and it remains to be seen who will be a part of this group...

We have learned a beautiful life lesson today in Varanasi. When we think about our impressions of this city and our uneasiness from this morning, we are faced with a new truth that surprises us: it is often when we go into the unknown that we are given beautiful moments to live. Fragility allows us to capture the most essential from life. Being true to oneself, living to the fullest, and having faith in life; that's what is truly important here.

Varanasi is certainly an enchanting land.

Day 41 – Sunday, October 19th, 2014
Varanasi – Calcutta, India

We wake up at dawn on this, our forty-first day of the adventure. We are meeting with Cyril and Itay at 5:30 sharp for a boat ride. Our early wake-up call is going to allow us to enjoy the calm and, most of all, the sunrise over the Ganges River.

Onboard a small boat, we slowly pull away from the riverbank as our guide rows away. The still slumbering Varanasi is outlined in ochre, purple, and brown; the misty Ganges is tinted in violet. During the two-hour ride, we observe every detail of this watercolor painting. The tranquility of the river transports us, and the slowly rising day fills us with energy.

Rays of sunlight soon appear, accompanied by a humidity that soon covers us like a cape. As we make our way back to the bank of the river, we try our hand at rowing: navigating on the Ganges River is a rare occurrence that we cannot miss.

Back on firm land, the beautiful Varanasi is now awake. The streets are buzzing with life again, even though their actions never really stopped. Once more, we delight in sampling the multiple culinary delights offered to us by the small shops, and we set off on a journey for our taste buds. We briefly cross paths with Sara, and decide to meet her later in the day.

Since leaving Paris, our encounters have been leading our progress, a fact even more noticeable in the Holy City. They light our path, and the personalities of each person we meet lead us to the unknown.

It is in this way that we find ourselves on the banks of the Ganges, ready to live through an incredible and impressive experience: bathing in the holy water. Milan and Cyril decline the offer... it is true that one needs to ignore the pollution, the filth, and the animal cadavers that we saw floating on the river during our morning ride. The idea, however, of letting go of apprehension and partaking in a Hindu belief ends up convincing Itay to join me.

Initiated by Sara and Emilia, we each jump into the "Mother Ganga". Though far from religious, the act has become symbolic to them. Marked by the spiritual ambiance, Emilia and Sara find this practice to be a way to contemplate their lives, to recenter, to meditate, and to be purified. This is a way to find spiritual and mental energy, and to continue along the path of full consciousness.

Touched by this event, we continue our time in the city by profiting from Emilia's wise words around a meal:
"The world needs love. Those who pursue material comforts are mistaken. We are on Earth to discover ourselves and others, and we can't do that through money."

A detachment from materialism, that's exactly what motivated our challenge, and crossing paths with other people who share this ideal is comforting to us. We leave the city with this thought in our minds.

Saying last goodbye to our guide, Debasish, we thank him for his hospitality and his presence. We then head to the train station where, after a two-hour delay, we take our seats on board the train heading to Calcutta. The atmosphere of the train is now familiar to us: the cars are all packed.

Diwali[12] is coming up soon, and many people are headed to-

12   'Diwali' or 'festival of lights' is one of the most popular festivals of Hinduism which extends over a five-day period where gifts are exchanged and fireworks are ignited.

ward the capital of West Bengal. There are also many students on the train today, as it is the end of their exam period. The trip promises to be epic: we are seated on a high seat, hunched up to avoid the menacing ceiling, our backs against the bars covering the windows and facing some fans... in this interesting position, we still attempt to have some conversations with our travel companions in order to lessen the impact of all the kilometers we have to travel. The hours pass, night falls, but sleep refuses to rock us in its gentle arms...

Day 42 – Monday, October 20th, 2014
Calcutta, India

Tossed around by the constant rocking of the train, hunched on the corner of a seat, or lying down on the floor next to the seats, on a bed of dust and cockroaches, we are desperate to fall asleep. When, by some sort of miracle, we do manage to drift off, we are shaken awake or made to move to another spot. This is an infernal cadence, slightly calmed by the appearance of the first rays of sunlight, which shine like some sort of signal of deliverance. Even though our traveling conditions are difficult, the powerful feeling of freedom that we feel since leaving Pakistan is still present.

Outside, the rice paddies stretch out as far as the eye can see, and the closer we get to Calcutta, the more dwellings and constructions multiply.

The heat and the crowd strike us once more as we get off at the train station. It is barely 9 in the morning but the temperature is already rather elevated and, without understanding where we are headed, we are carried off by the flow of the people walking alongside the traffic.

The immensity of the city is disconcerting. It is going to be difficult to find the right path and impossible to hitchhike between the unending lines of taxis and buses.

After a heap of questions without answers, we manage to obtain some information and, a couple negotiations later, we are finally on a bus headed toward the City Center. The bus drops us off after a long ride, and imagine our surprise when we realize that the famous City Center isn't the downtown, but a new and flamboyant shopping mall on the outskirts of Calcutta. It seems like fate is a prankster...

Far from being defeated by this detour, we throw ourselves into the walkways of the center, and our optimism pays off rather quickly. We run into Deep and Vikash who, after learning of our project, put us into a taxi and give us a precious address.

It is in this way that we meet Iftekhar. Smiling and welcoming, this young father and owner of a business which organizes guided tours of the city, Calcutta Walks, immediately stops what he is doing to occupy himself with our care. This is a sort of hospitality like no other!

We leave his office and follow him to discover the city. While walking through the streets, we remember Iran and Germany, which he has also visited, due to the warmth of the people and the particularity of their environments. A Muslim man, Iftekhar talks to us about Buddhism and then, when we're in the English-Speaking quarter, he reminds us of the colonial past, an important chapter in the history of India. He also tells us about the old governmental regimes like communism, of which there are still traces here and there, such as the blood red floating in the wind.

When we mention media and the press, Iftekhar immediately lights up and whips out his phone to call one of his contacts at a newspaper, The Telegraph, certain that our adventure will interest him.

After this completely impromptu interview – which is certainly welcome since the visibility brought about by a newspaper article can help us find a sponsor to help us reach Thailand either by cargo vehicle or by plane – our host opens the doors to his family home. While he plays with and hugs his twin children, a girl and a boy only a few months old, he cannot resist but to complain about the educational system in the country:

"I hope that my children won't have to live through this systemic categorization that reduces the freedom of all people. It is my responsibility as a parent to make sure this doesn't happen. I want each of them to be free to explore their full potential."

His confessions, his availability, and his trust in us are signs that our challenge and our adventure are not carried out in vain. Day after day, the goodwill in each person we meet allows us to advance and to live wonderful moments based on sharing. In each one of the stages of this trip, we delightfully plunge into the multiple cultural identities we meet and face the realities they face, as different or as difficult as they may be.

We go back outside. The day is fading and there are still tons of people in the streets, but this isn't too surprising considering that Calcutta has the highest population density in the entire country. Curious and amused, we witness the life of the Bengalis: the walking merchants, the still-infernal traffic, and the small group of men crowded around a card game.

After a discussion from earlier in the day about cinema, Iftekhar sends us off to watch a film while he takes care of some business. Even though we're thrilled with the idea, the Hindi[13] adaptation of Hamlet soon gets the best of us. In order to not fall into a deep sleep, we decide to answer the call of the streets, which are more attractive than the cinema hall. Our wanderings lead us through darkened alleys and illuminated avenues, from a repair workshop to a rice and spice shop.

Afterwards, we are joined by Iftekhar and his brother-in-law, Dabish, and we continue our trek through the city until we reach the home of the latter, where we are greeted like kings. The succulent meal and the musical ambiance charm us, and we go to sleep full and happy.

Day 43 – Tuesday, October 21st, 2014
Calcutta, India

Forty-third day of the challenge, and ninth day in India. We have spent a long night full of refreshing sleep, and we arise as excited as two children on Christmas Day – and on the eve of Diwali, the Festival of Lights that is akin to the end of year celebration in the Western Year, this is not completely abnormal behavior! – at the idea of opening today's edition of The Telegraph, which prints two million daily copies. We are very disappointed, though, when we don't find our article in the pages of the newspaper...

We quickly forget this, though, as we experience the events of the day.

---

13   'Hindi' is the official language of India.

Our host, Dabish, whose hospitality and availability rival those of Iftekhar, seems to be invested in our mission. On top of offering us room and board, for which we are very grateful, he also offers us a guided tour of his city, sharing anecdotes and details about the place.

Calcutta is intriguing and fascinating due to its touristic dimension. Its heritage and great cultural and intellectual richness make it one of the most attractive cities in India, and its industrial sector is also striking. When we approach the economic center of the city, Dabish tells us that each street is dedicated to a certain craft or skill. Be it textiles, furniture, technology, or steel works, each workshop and merchant is effectively grouped by theme.

The owner of a family-run business, Dabish leads us excitedly to his store, happy to be able to share his knowledge and accomplishments. In the middle of an infinite number of boxes and pairs of sandals, a narrow table acting as an office allows him to masterfully manage his business. He is a generous master, as well, as he offers us each a pair of sandals without thinking twice.

Throughout the whole day, we discover the astounding streets of Calcutta. Here, we taste syrupy pastries, and there, we visit one of the most ancient mosques in the city. During our wanderings through the brick and jade alcoves, we stumble upon a grandiose open-air hall. The daylight reflects off the peaceful surface of the fountains, and the place is perfect for religious ritual washing.

Our walk continues and we are soon joined by Iftekhar and Vikash, one of his friends who will be hosting us tonight. We live at the rhythm of our Bengali friends: drinking fresh coconut milk, watching a carrom ball ("poor man's billiards") tournament, eating at only the best of the food stands...

Even though we still don't know how we're going to reach Bangkok – working in exchange for tickets seems to be in vain – we consider ourselves lucky to have the support and the devotion of our hosts.

Our worries, though, are quickly put into perspective.

Calcutta is full of paradoxes. From the pomp and splendor of the ancient British Raj and the shining examples of culture and intellect to misery there is but one step. Once night has fallen and the hordes of pedestrians, workers, students, and cars thin out, the misery becomes visible, no matter how well-hidden it is during the day. The poor and the homeless wander around looking for a meal or for a place to sleep. While some wash up in the stagnant water of the gutters, others don't leave their section of sidewalk, their piece of sheet metal, or their wooden pallet, their only mattresses for the night.

Bangkok, the Thai jewel, seems very far away tonight as the lights go out on this rather particular day. From the heights of our building, sheltered in Vikash's office, we are filled with the feeling of being immensely privileged.

43 DAYS = 11 938KM

INDIA

Amritsar

PAKISTAN

New Delhi

Agra (Taj Mahal)

Mahoba

Jhansi
Orchha   Varanasi
        Chhatarpur

Calcutta

INDIA

Day 44 – Wednesday, October 22nd, 2014
Calcutta, India – Bangkok, Thailand

"Magic exists." These are the words pronounced by Iftekhar when summing up this magnificent day, a day marked by good fortune.

Full of the contradictory images that we've witnessed since the beginning of this adventure, and especially in the last few days in India, the intentions of our challenge are even bigger. We can't ignore the poverty and the hardships of life that we've observed and of which we rub shoulders with every day. At the same time, the generosity and kindness that we've been shown make humanity a non-isolated quality. Above any question of religion, this faith in humankind is a common value that we must keep in mind and share. In terms of our challenge, this means that we have to continue forward.

The race against the clock has started. We have already tried to get in touch with airlines and travel agencies during the last few days, and we've proposed our photographic or directorial services, among others. All without success.

Today, we are going to explore all our possibilities. Maybe new encounters today or our network will lead us to Bangkok. Who knows?

The day begins at full speed. The article we were promised appears on the Metro supplement of The Telegraph, in an insert on the first page, accompanied with a photo of our duo. It is disconcerting to see ourselves in a foreign newspaper, but it is nothing compared to what awaits us. This sudden distinction, as ephemeral as it may be, elicits many sympathetic responses and encouragements from the passersby as we walk through the streets. Now that we're on people's minds, we have to try and not disappoint.

Excitement, joy, doubt, empathy... we are feeling a whole range of emotions, and we are hypersensitive to everything that happens. However, not too long after, we have barely sat down in front of a computer to attack our problem when we see a message of salvation appear on our screen: "we will pay for your tickets".

Six words, no more, no less. Is this a joke? False hope? Maybe, maybe not.

Without a second thought, we strike up a conversation with this mysterious messenger. He seems sure of himself and his proposition. This is good. We call him, our heart rate increasing with each ring of the tone. We set up a meeting later on, and we jump out of our chairs in joy. Bangkok is dizzyingly approaching.

This is followed by a calculation of kilometers, distances, of days remaining, and of estimations... welcome to the behind-the-scenes of Optimistic Traveler. Everything gets confused and mixed up; when do we leave? The choice is difficult, since we're torn between the call of the road and of the challenge, and the invitation we've received to attend the Diwali festivities. Our dilemma is solved by our benefactor, Amit Sarogi, a businessman with whom we share many values. Tickets in hand, we are now leaving to Bangkok tonight at midnight. The idea is thrilling but the timing is tight. Between the meal shared with Amit's family and our return to Iftekhar's house to pick up our things, we don't have a second to lose. We toss our freshly washed and still wet clothing in plastic bags and we head toward the airport. Amit's driver weaves between the traffic and gets us there in record time. We squeeze out our clothes in front of the airport while we wait for our departure. This has been an unforgettable night, even though we haven't managed to charge our cameras and film the events.

This last encounter ends our chapter in India. We turn the page on Calcutta, but we keep in our minds the memories of the relationships that we've formed with our hosts and friends. The gratitude that we feel for them and their generous actions is eternal.

And so, borrowing Iftekhar's words: magic definitely does exist.

Day 45 – Thursday, October 23rd, 2014
Bangkok, Thailand

After a handful of hours on a plane we arrive in Southeast Asia, one more jump across the world map. We just traveled across 2000 kilometers as easily as pawns slide across a game board. We can't complain; on the contrary, we savor the beginning of this new round.

This debut is a tad slow, though. It is 5 in the morning and the public transport lines are still not running, so we have to wait for a while before we can go downtown. Thanks to a young German man who buys us the first ticket, and a Thai woman visiting her sister from Paris, who buys us the second, we are ready to go.

Once in the metropolis, the change of décor is striking. The sprawling city is a mass of concrete, and the highways and buildings make us dizzy. We're in another world, one in a different dimension and with a different ambiance.

The climate here is also destabilizing. The humidity is overwhelming, and each movement feels heavy. We drip sweat each step we take. The incomprehension that we feel when interacting with the people we meet is also troubling. Very few individuals can speak English, and even though we are greeted warmly and with smiles, it is difficult to glean any sort of useful information or precise directions. Our project – that of collaborating with others – is easy to doubt at this moment, and when we mention it to people we are directed either to temples or to the police.

Exhausted, we take shelter in what seems to be a park next to a busy avenue. We soon learn that it is, in fact, a hippodrome attached to a golf course, both part of a hotel complex not far from here. It doesn't matter to us, and we continue on our path. When we reach a thicket, we stumble upon a small restaurant kiosk run by a family. When they see our desperate faces, they take pity on our situation and feed us bowls of rice and hot eggs. With our stomachs now full, and our wet clothes now hanging from a cord between two trees, we throw ourselves on the grass to take a nap, not woken up by even the oppressive heat until many hours later.

Now that we've had enough of a break, we need to continue along our path. In a square, there are many groups forming, and our curiosity leads us to them. The families set up plastic mats on the sidewalk and sit in front of the street. There are garlands of white jasmine, yellow saffron, and pink roses everywhere, and the smoke from many sticks of incense fills the air. The reason? The fervor provoked by the national celebration of King Chulalongkorn, and the procession in his honor that is to take place in this street. The neighborhood, roped off for the occasion, isn't going to be helpful to our journey, and we leave, following directions that we obtain here and there.

Bangkok is now before our very eyes. In this tourist neighborhood, the traditional architecture mixes with the more modern buildings, the roofs of the temples here and there pierce the sky, and there are tourists and traveling merchants milling around an endless amount of restaurants, bars, and hotels.

Our tentative requests for lodging are refused, but we press on, as usual. With a bit of time, optimism succeeds and we find opportunities. We meet Robert, a German tourist of Russian descent, who has just arrived in Thailand on a five-week adventure. Armed with his smile and his big arms, he immediately offers to buy us a drink and then, after some reflection, decides to share his room with us. And there you have it: a coffee and a bed are all we need to restore our happiness after twelve hours of uncertainty. Even though the idea of spending time with locals is still our first priority, the community of travelers that we come across allows us to look at our experience in a different light.

Relieved of our backpacks and refreshed after a shower, we leave with our new companion to seek out the nightlife of the city. Later, when we're seated around a table, two people passing by recognize Muammer and call out to him. Two French men, Antoine and Martin, or Clic and Clac as they're nicknamed, are also traveling around the world. Passionate about adventures, they learned about ours on the internet, as crazy as that may sound.

Our exchanges and the sharing of stories make this evening seem festive and cosmopolitan. They are soon joined by their friends, fascinating people they've met here and there during their travels, and we let ourselves be carried away by each encounter, again and again.

113

Day 46 – Friday, October 24th, 2014
Bangkok – Chumphon, Thailand

There are three of us in this tiny dark room. No windows. No ventilation. A simple bed for two of us. These are conditions that aren't optimal for rest, but we still appreciate them. After all the nights spent on the hard floors of the trains in India, nothing seems too little for us now.

Robert, as generous as always, takes us to eat a large breakfast outside. After two heavy showers, the rainy season being almost at its end, we take advantage of the weather to pick up our things from the hotel and take them a little farther to our new shelter.

The weather, now better than before, is conducive to exploring and discovering the city on foot. The cultural and artistic heritage of Thailand consists mainly of religious art, and so we take advantage of our time outside to soak up as much of it as we can. The bright colors and the shiny gold detailing catch out eyes and fascinate us. The temples are full of images of serpents, ornaments in the shape of birds, lotuses, and other sacred motifs, and the architectural symbolism is inspired by Hindu-Buddhist iconography. After catching these sights, it is a Chinese temple that attracts our attention.

The promenade continues onboard a long-tail boat on the canals of the city, an activity once again proposed by our acolyte. From the river, we observe the city life and habits from another angle.

We disembark at Chinatown, another face of Bangkok. The racks of fruit and vegetables, food, accessories, of gadgets of all

114

sorts, the shops and the restaurants one after the other, this all reminds us that we're currently in an Asian metropolis. As in every touristy neighborhood, the appeal to consume is almost overwhelming. We take a bit of time to try a steaming soup seated at a table jutting out of a street food stand, but we don't take long before getting back on our boat and heading back to the hotel.

It is now 4 in the afternoon. With our backpacks on, we face a slight argument, not the first one of the day. We hope we don't continue to go down this slippery slope.

Staying in Bangkok, as I've suggested, or leaving the city to change our environment, as Muammer has proposed... that is the question.

We look to obtain information about the bus heading to Chumphon. The schedules are all nocturnal, but we recognize that if we do the ten hour trip at night we'll gain many kilometers. Taking advantage of the Wi-Fi in the lobby of our hotel, I see a message from my friend Stephan, whom I consider to be almost like a brother. He is currently living on the island of Koh Tao, close to Chumphon. Seeing an opportunity to meet up and share my adventure with him, the motivation to leave Bangkok suddenly comes back to me.

Our disagreement is now snuffed out, and we leave Robert with heavy hearts. A young Thai woman leads us to the public transport and helps us get easily to the bus terminal.

Here, our usual quest recommences: we need to find someone to buy us tickets. The station is enormous, and it throws us off. We look around the ticket booths hoping to find sponsors, doubling our efforts, but no one seems to want to help us. The situation finally comes to an end thanks to two foreigners in transit who graciously buy us our tickets. We can now add Finland and Russia to our list of countries that have cooperated in our challenge.

Tickets now in our hands, we wait for our bus to arrive, and our wait goes by very quickly while we have a discussion with a nearby Quebecois man. We hear the final call to board the bus toward Chumphon, and we leave the city.

Day 47 - Saturday, October 25th, 2014
Chumphon - Koh Tao, Thailand

The asphalt zooms by as we ride the bus under the starlight, and we arrive in Chumphon before the sun comes up. Numb with cold due to the Arctic-like conditions inside the bus, we're happy when we step into the pleasantly humid environment outside. Our happiness doesn't last for long since our day begins on the wrong note. Was it the rough night? Did we both wake up on the wrong side of the bed? Or is it the disagreement from last night that awoke between us? We'll soon know, since the Optimistic Traveler duo isn't acting in unison today, as we fiercely debate about how to continue the adventure.

With the challenge in his mind, Muammer wants to go as fast as we can to Malaysia. On the other hand, the call of nature and meeting with Stephan are my biggest motivations for today. We talk for hours and neither one of us budges.

Are we going to waste our time spending our day on the island of Koh Tao? Are we breaking the rules of our challenge by visiting a friend? Is the choice that we're making really realistic or are we simply trying to fulfill a pleasure?

A shadow is cast over this paradisiacal environment that we're in. This is a wrong step, yes, but it is one that reflects something other than just a simple disagreement.

This project, this journey around the world in eighty days, is far from being anodyne. It was born out of personal desires and initiatives, even though it is carried out with other people in mind. Our aspirations and our beliefs make up the base of our association. The encounters, names, faces, words, and smiles fill us every day and carry us a little farther each time, allowing us to get closer to our objective.

These strong moments touch and rattle us at the same time. We receive so many welcoming gestures that, when we're alone, our emotions are sometimes put to the test, one that can sometimes allow for certain less-than-savory aspects of our personalities come out. A negative side to all the positive ones.

The state of mind that we find ourselves in now, on this forty-seventh day, is decidedly similar to those of most of the people we meet today. When we finally arrive on Koh Tao, surrounded by the French-Canadians we met last night and by Stephan and his friends, we realize something: there is no one here, at the end of the world. In this beautiful place, worthy of a postcard, motivated by a desire to escape from their lives, everyone tries to harmonize with their ideas, with their ideologies. We are alone in these processes, true, but we all came here together thanks to something: our passion for nature and its discovery. And what better way to express these than to go diving?

Beyond being a simple activity, diving is about going beyond oneself, physically and mentally, and uniting the body and soul. It is about re-energizing oneself.

The soft undulating of the waves rocks us and we record these instants, these inspirations, in our minds. On the beach, I take advantage of this moment of serenity to express to Muammer all of my gratitude for his understanding of my choices and his support. The black night envelops Koh Tao, and the strange day finally reaches its end. Pacified and reassured by the positive energy we've rediscovered, we fall into a deep sleep.

Day 48 – Sunday, October 26th, 2014
Koh Tao – Hat Yai, Thailand

Waking up is pleasant on the island of Koh Tao. The idyllic landscapes, the clear warm water, and the coral reefs full of underwater life are prime tourist attractions in the area. The crossroads of many travelers with fascinating stories, Koh Tao knows how to use its charms to seduce the adventurous souls searching for some well-being.

We are invited to dinner by the delightful Marine, who is stationed on this island while training to be a diving instructor, and we take advantage of the moment to profit from her presence, our host's, and of the surrounding quietness. Koh Tao hypnotizes and charms us to the point of forgetting our departure time. We have a final surprise on the island when Robert, in the flesh, is in front of us, also looking to enjoy diving on the island. We share a coffee with him, and after hugging him goodbye, we quickly get on the boat. The boat company doesn't resist giving us the tickets for free after finding out about challenge (and after we mischievously slid some candy under their eyes!). This is a generous gesture, and it is accompanied with enthusiastic smiles.

Back on the mainland in Chumphon at the beginning of the afternoon, we hurry to find out what we must do to go to the next place on our list: Hat Yai, almost 600 kilometers from here. Based on the advice that we've received from travelers and expatriates, hitchhiking isn't going to be helpful in this region, and we decide to ride the train. The next one leaves at 9 PM, so we have a lot of time to organize ourselves. We hope that we'll continue to be as lucky as we've been until now!

As is customary for us now, we set out looking for restaurants and shops where we can meet people. We also try to go against the common idea in Thailand that when people leave the tourist centers it is difficult to be understood.

From one place to another, the reception we are given is completely different. When they throw us out of one place for using their Wi-Fi without consuming anything, we are invited to another place to eat. As to our train tickets, many people are very open and honest about their impossibility to help us. Salaries in this region of the world aren't very high, and we don't insist.

It is the turn of North America to play the role of benefactor. Lauren and Laura, two young women who have been working in the field of humanitarianism for several months, come to our aid. Curious, funny, wise, and full of life, they are savoring their trip and their experiences, becoming conscious of the enriching nature of the world that they are benefiting from. We attentively listen to everything they say.

After this intense moment, we take different paths once more. Calmed down by the events of the evening, we decide to give back what has been given to us. Taking advantage of the internet connection in a hostel, we officially launch our fundraising campaign for Haiti Care[14], an existing association that we've decided to support. This is a project near and dear to our hearts that we want to share with the world, and this is a significant first step.

Euphoric, we gather our things and head to the train station. On our way, we cross Carole and Claire, two German women, with whom we celebrate the good news. Though they are a bit taken aback by our enthusiasm, they gladly join us and buy us some mango sticky rice to celebrate the moment before we set off again.

The train blows its whistle, marking its departure. We take our seats on board, and we delightedly discover a bunk reserved for each of us. How fancy! What a way to spend another night on journeying across the other side of the world...

Day 49 – Monday, October 27th, 2014
Hat Yai, Thailand

The sun rises over the Thai peninsula. The mangrove forests, dense and humid, surround the train tracks and line the coast, and cover us with a delicate green hue. The rays of sunlight pierce the thick canopy here and there, and blind us with their bright shine.

We reach the Hat Yai train station early in the morning, before 7. It is not too early, however, for the street traders to be selling their wares from carts all along the main street. This is a typical scene in an Asian country, one that never ceases to

---

14   'Haiti Care' is an international organization, implemented since
      15 years in Haiti. Its team of 6 persons launch and follow up
      development programs and participate in rebuilding the
      country as it is heavily effected by seismism, cholera, ...

surprise us, but that is slowly becoming familiar. Andrey, our neighbor on the train, buys us "breakfast", a coffee and chips, before setting off on his way. We should do the same, since we also have a long way to go today.

We are 15,000 kilometers from Paris, and we don't know why we are in the small city of Hat Yai other than the fact that it is on the way to Malaysia. Either way, we hope that we are going to be able to change the way we've been functioning the last few days and maybe Hat Yai will hold the answer.

We run into many foreigners, each more interesting than the last, and all supportive of our adventure. Their help is precious to us, and we advance quite a bit thanks to them. We are far from home, though, and we want to be able to meet some of the locals and exchange with them. We hold our memories of the moments we passed with families in Iran or in India close to our hearts, and we would love to be able to have more of these on the last part of our trip through Thailand.

The day is difficult, as the hesitations, refusals, and misunderstandings pile up. We strike up several conversations with some of the locals, even share pleasant moments around a drink or a meal, but the connection isn't really there and the hope of finding a place to stay tonight fades away slowly.

In the late afternoon, the day is falling and we still haven't found a place to stay. Hat Yai is mostly calm and we are afraid of not being able to find a solution. Following the advice of a couple, we try going to the temples but, like in Bangkok, we are turned away for reasons independent from people's generosity. The first one is undergoing renovations and can't host anyone, and the second, a Chinese temple, doesn't host anyone but monks. We are disappointed, but happy about being able to look at this beautiful architecture once more.

Defeated, we plonk down on the terrace of a restaurant. Without much hope, we begin a conversation with a Thai couple seated next to us. While we're chatting, the exchanges multiply and they eventually invite us to stay at their home. We are saved!

A few minutes from there, we discover a beautiful wine-colored house that masterfully combines modern and traditional architecture. The surprises don't stop there; Kung and Ya have been coy about their profession, and when they finally reveal that they have rooms to let, we are overjoyed to see that they are opening up one of them to us. We are certainly being treated like princes here!

Once we're set up, we see Kung coming to take us to a sports hall, where we play memorable badminton matches with his friends, his father, and his brother. These are just more unforgettable moments to add to our collection.

The rest of the evening passes by in a similar fashion. We spend hours sitting on the terrace in front of the house, talking about respective projects and lives. Their warm reception of us is a beautiful reflection of their family life with their son Get: simple, attentive, and loving. What more could we want from this final evening in Thailand?

We are already full of memories, but we didn't expect the arrival of Andrew, the British gentleman bitten by the travel bug, who is staying in the same place as us. We had met him earlier in the day and didn't expect to see him again. What a shame that would have been! His composure and his humor add a touch of elegance to this already delightful evening.

Tuesday, September 9th: we set off from Eiffel Tower.

Passing by Munich.

We search for a ride to Vienna... and we find one!

Waking up in the magnificent mosque in Ankara.

On the roof of the mosque.

Two of our Turkish drivers.

At the home of our Turkish professors.

A diabolo show.

One of our hosts.

Grooming ourselves at the Iranian border...

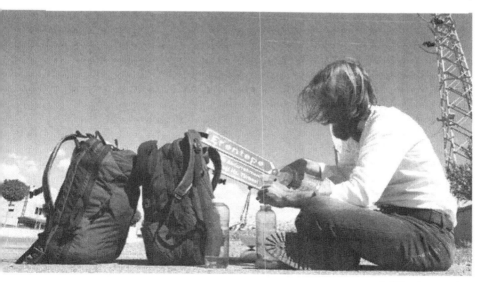

...and filtering water.

In Erzurum,
interviewed
while we wait
for our visas.

Last glance
at Turkey.

Other travelers stranded in Erzurum.

The time has come to continue our journey.

Finally, Iran.

In the Grand Bazaar of Isfahan.

First Leili and then Sima opened their doors for us.

Family meal in Yazd during the Festival of Sacrifice (Kurban Bayrami).

On the bus, near the Pakistan border.

Last cautions before reaching
the border.

We are well escorted as we enter Pakistan.

In Lahore, a brief visit to the barber.

On the train to Lahore, another universe.

In New Delhi.

In front of the entrance to the Taj Mahal, Agra.

We arrive in
Varanasi.

Ritualistic
ceremony
along the
Ganges.

We´re in the newspaper!

Morning boat ride on the Ganges.

In Calcutta,
showers are
taken outside,
on the street.

Short nap in
Bangkok.

Thai cuisine
is simply
delicious.

With Stephan,
on Koh Tao
Island.

A vacation
day on this
paradise
island.

Buddha.

We arrive in Malaysia.

Hitchhiking in Kuala Lumpur is a real challenge.

At the Singapore zoo.

Thanks to Anahita, we have our tickets to the USA!

J.B. Wood hosts us in
San Francisco.

The California coast.

Warm greetings in
Salt Lake City.

We look over the city at sunset.

On board the California Zephyr.

In Denver.

We meet Melissa.

In Chicago, with Joe.

Painting session.

On the train, Muammer pursues his childhood dream.

In New York, we visit the UN.

We are in Marrakesh, our adventure almost complete.

In Casablanca, in front of the Grand Mosque with Mohammed, Nahima, and their three daughters.

On the road
to Tangier
with Yasin.

We hitchhike to Spain to reach France.

Last day before reaching Paris.

In Paris, we stay with Antoine de Maximy.

Paris, our last stop with Valeria, Didier, and their children.

We arrive at the Champs-Élysées by hitchhiking.

The end of our journey at the foot of the Eiffel Tower.

We celebrate our return with Léa at the bistro.

DU MONDE SANS UN CENTIME !

We are interviewed on the Grand Journal on Canal +.

Day 50 – Tuesday, October 28th, 2014
Hat Yai, Thailand – Kuala Lumpur, Malaysia

It is hard for us to get out of bed in the morning. The memories of last night and the sumptuous comfort of our room keep us in a blissful half-awake state. When we finally manage to get up, we discover, stunned, the last presents from Andrew: a bag filled with food, dried mangoes, chocolate bars, bread, and all sorts of snacks. We can subsist on these the whole day! The proclaimed English Optimistic Traveler ambassador is definitely taking his role to heart.

We find our hostess in the lobby of the guest house. As attentive as always, she proffers two bottles of water, and proposes to drive us with her husband to the highway leading to Malaysia. Before dropping us off, they insist showing us one last place: from the heights of his pedestal, a dazzling gold statue of Buddha watches over the city. We savor this idyllic and incomparable view over Hat Yai in the company of our friends. Afterward, we continue along our challenge that is now leading us to reach Kuala Lumpur by hitchhiking.

Once we pass over the language barrier – it is difficult to make people understand our destination when the writing and pronunciation of city names is different in English and Thai – we quickly find a vehicle to ride in. We barely manage to escape the torrential rain that suddenly downpours from above us and are relieved to be under a roof. Our driver, hesitant at first to pick up two hitchhikers, finally accepts to take us all the way to the Malaysian border. We leave her car, get on a tractor trailer, and our excitement rises when we see the border posts. Our driver drops us off in front of customs, and the verification of our papers goes by without a hitch. We are now in Malaysia, with yet another visa stamp in our passports!

The challenge continues. We have some trouble finding a strategic point to facilitate the approach of vehicles. Trucks, trailers, sedans, buses, and many other vehicles pass by without stopping. Powerless and annoyed, we watch them all fade away, but we cannot let this beat us, and we refuse to let the situation continue like this.

Muammer finds another spot, and I set off to chase a bus. Good news soon reaches our ears.

Our new benefactor is named Rusli. A Thai man living in Malaysia, Rusli is traveling by coach to Kuala Lumpur, and he agrees to pay for our tickets after he hears my speech. Other passengers participate and help him out by contributing funds, something that we had never witnessed until now. We continue to be amazed by everything we observe during this trip. When we board the coach and talk about our search for a place to stay for the night, Rusli volunteers once again. His sparkling gaze and his reassuring smile become our companions on the road today.

For a few hours, we ride on the coach heading south. Near midnight, the shining towers of Kuala Lumpur light up the night sky, and we soon arrive in the sleeping city.

A short taxi ride later and we're diving into Rusli's universe. It is a surprising mix of bikers with big hearts, as his friends are all passionate about Harley-Davidson motorcycles, and an ever-present family environment. Everyone here is extremely welcoming. His younger brother, an experienced graphic designer, stops what he is doing and dedicates all his time to make sure that we're cared for. In the blink of an eye, he begins drawing portraits of us in the Manga style, with expert

140

strokes of a pencil. Impressive! His pencil strokes capture us perfectly.

Day 51 – Wednesday, October 29th, 2014
Kuala Lumpur, Malaysia

Given that we've traveled many kilometers in one day, and that we're currently on top of our schedule, we decide to spend the day visiting the city.

Kuala Lumpur is a fascinating place. With its sparkling steel towers, its endless amounts of skyscrapers, its shopping malls, and luxurious boutiques it makes us feel like we're in another dimension. The humidity in the air is but a faint memory while we're walking through the streets, or rather, the walkways, which are enclosed and air-conditioned paths. We have never seen anything like it.

The gap between the neighborhoods far away from the financial center are quite large but the city functions regardless, and seems to work well this way. When we ask the citizens about their lifestyles and the quality of their lives, their response is unanimous. The important thing one must do in order to enjoy the city's attractions is to work, and once you're busy everything seems like it's OK. Inequalities certainly are visible here and there, but the zest for life we witness today doesn't reveal any negative aspects. Inactivity is not on the program for Kuala Lumpur.

A crossroads of Malayasian, Indian, and Chinese culture, the city presents those cosmopolitan influences in its architecture, its cuisine, and in the arts. Stimulating and dynamic, Kuala Lumpur surprises and amazes, much like the encounters that we have there.

While walking around designer shops, we run into Martin Stevenson, the English author of the book More than Footprints, and editor-in-chief of a website of the same name, seated on the terrace of a café. Absorbed by his work on the computer, he lifts his head and gives us five minutes of his time, which then turn into a long discussion about the evolution of mass tourism and the necessity of a more responsible form of tourism that can counterbalance the negative side effects. This is an unexpected and constructive exchange that we appreciate immensely.

Later on in the day, after many fruitless attempts to visit the Petronas Towers, an intriguing reinforced steel construction, we manage to get invited to the top floor of the KL Tower, also called the Menara Kuala Lumpur, thanks to an Indian family who buys us the entry tickets. The view from here is impressive. The city and its gleaming sparkles spread out beneath us, and to make this moment even better, we meet Victor. The French student, passionate about traveling, is journeying along across South East Asia. His good mood, his liveliness, his reaction to our description of our challenge, and the way he immediately launches into flagging down a taxi, Optimistic Traveler style, all make us smile in joy. We enjoy his presence so much that after spending the evening with him we invite him to Singapore the next day.

His response, almost immediate, was unexpected. Victor is officially joining our team for the next stage of our journey!

"I'll just fetch my passport and I'll follow you!"

We separate on those happy words, excited to see him tomorrow. We return, delighted with our day's events, to Rusli and his family's home, and they are happy to host us for a second night.

Day 52 – Thursday, October 30th, 2014
Kuala Lumpur, Malaysia – Republic of Singapore

Even during a journey on the other side of the world, it is extraordinary to see how much one can create new habits and customs. On this second day in Kuala Lumpur, today begins just like yesterday, in the small restaurant in front of the house we're staying in, managed by Rusli's mother and twin brother. Victor, our new companion, joins us to share a plate of rice vegetables prepared carefully by the cook. We now have the energy needed to, all three together, face this new challenge that awaits us.

Leaving a large agglomeration such as this one is something that we've done before, but that does not make it easy. After several refusals and hesitations, a pedestrian helps us out by buying three tickets for a bus that will take us to the outskirts of the city. Once we're set up at the first service station accessible to us, we begin our favorite dance, animated by our favorite tune, to try to convince the drivers passing by to pick us up.

About twenty cars go by and not a single one accepts this proposal, and our failure stings. The situation gets a little more complicated when the manager of the station asks us to leave before he calls the police.

Muammer and Victor comply, while I present our case to the manager.

My arguments seem to dissuade him from carrying out his threat, and he picks up the phone to call not the police, but a taxi who he pays to take us to the highway leading to Singapore. First victory.

New rest stop, new hopes. Quickly, Muammer confirms these positive energies when he convinces Mr. Lam to pick us up in his sedan. Armed with a selection of coffee, chai tea, and cakes he has given us, we head south to Tangkak. Originally from this region, Mr. Lam can't take us any farther, but it doesn't mean that his generosity stops here. Before sending us off on a bus to complete the second half of our trip, he takes us out first for a meal and then to try one of the most expensive and rare delicacies in South East Asia: swallow's nest. Although we are disconcerted by the idea of the dish and the bland flavor, we accept the challenge. We've heard that these nests are well-known for their health benefits, and on top of that, we can't let such a unique experience pass us by.

The 150 kilometers that separate us from our destination go by in the blink of an eye, and we rapidly approach the island of Singapore. We change buses before we walk through what seem to be hallways, walkways, and halls taken directly out of an airport in order to enter this new territory. Finally, we arrive in the Republic of Singapore.

Well, almost. We are slightly delayed at the border post, because Muammer's trips through Africa raise health concerns, and because we don't have plane tickets, hotel reservations, or money, and this naturally intrigues the authorities. We are plunged into uncertainty and time goes by slowly. Finally, though, the media trail documenting our adventure are proof enough that we are telling the truth, and we are let through.

Finally: the Republic of Singapore.

We reach the downtown thanks to Pauline, a young French-woman who buys us public transport tickets. Futuristic buildings appear before our surprised eyes as we ride in the bus. It is now dark outside and the lights of endless buildings illuminate the night sky. We leave our ride and walk around one of these attractive complexes, guided only by our instinct.

Be it by good luck, a twist of fate, or simple coincidence, we don't know, but our challenge has taught us each day that there are lessons to be learned everywhere, and that we must apply them using our instinct and open-mindedness. Sometimes, luck is on our side and we must go with the flow. Marvi Farkoush, his wife Anahita, and their son, a charming Iranian family, are our lucky twist of fate today. They are walking through the same area at the same time we are, and in the fraction of a second we establish contact. A simple exchange leads to a long and rich discussion around drinks. We talk about the stakes of education, and equality, and we discuss our convictions and desires. We are deeply moved by this evening, filled with their presence, the time that they dedicate to us, and their financial investment, all of which become precious memories.

From the heights of our golden tower – because our guardian angels have insisted on paying for a room in a five-star hotel despite our attempts to dissuade them – we think about the events of the day and about the trek we have made. From the largest gesture to the smallest action, everything counts. Even though we appreciate our fancy surroundings for the night, our vision, our perception of gifts, and of the goodwill we receive remain unchanged.

As to Victor, well, he's starry eyed thinking about every moment we've lived today. He confesses that he barely slept last night, worried about what was to come, but the magic of our day has given him back his confidence, to the point where he promises us that he himself will take a journey like this one day.

Days 53 to 56 – Friday, October 31st to Monday, November 3rd, 2014, Republic of Singapore

We are here. The big leap, the big crossing, the one that we've been waiting for since the beginning of this journey: the Pacific Ocean.

Taking off, flying to the other side of the globe. If only we could turn back the clock... but no, the West Coast of the United States is waiting for us with arms wide open. It would be a shame to stop when we're on such a good path.

We are here. The moment of truth. We prove, time and time again, that humanity can be found in every corner of the planet, even though we constantly see only the negative. But, is generosity similarly without limits?

These tickets, we want them in order to be able to complete this challenge, this adventure that is now more than just a personal desire, but an initiative to launch our humanitarian dreams. Beyond this gesture, the formative experience is revealing an attitude with which we face life in general.

Four days. It took us four days to obtain our precious golden tickets. Four long days filled with highs and lows, passing from enthusiasm to disappointment. From doubt to hope. Ninety-six hours that rocked us like a rollercoaster.

Making the decision on the first morning to leave the bubble that was our hotel room and letting Victor go wasn't easy to do. We all get accustomed quickly to comfort, no matter how fleeting it may be. But alas, we launch ourselves into our new mission, spending hours in the hallways of the airport and the downtown travel agencies only to see the doors close in front of us and our opportunities to leave Asia diminishing with every refusal. Presenting Optimistic Traveler as a marketing plan isn't something that gives us pleasure, but a second's hesitation can be fatal. We are then further destabilized when, accepting an invitation to a rugby game on Saturday, we find ourselves in front of an ocean of businessmen, all expatriates or members of the high Singaporean society, and none of them really open for discussion. Even though our host's invitation came from a good place – he thought that sharing his contacts and his network would help us find a solution – we quickly feel uncomfortable. Exchanging and speaking about our project here has turned into begging, and we don't like this one bit. This is a strange sensation, and we leave that place soon after.

Is this going to defeat us? Definitely not; the bad experiences that live through mean almost nothing in the face of the encouragements, the affection, and the connections that we make. We must not forget the little gestures here and there, and always set out to discover them.

If Victor, who traveled with us for one day, had the impression that the world and many possibilities were spread before him, how can we, with fifty days behind us, see otherwise?

Like yin and yang, the negative energies go hand in hand with the positive ones. When Louis, one of the managers of Singapore Airlines, announces to us that he can't make a decision about a sponsor for our tickets, we realize quickly that our optimism and our willpower, as well as our challenge, must be shared.

There are certain words that resonate with us and stay in our subconscious. Words that come and confirm an intuition, and words that simply comfort us. Sometimes, everything is connected; all the signs, the sly wink of an eye, the chance encounters. How can we not smile and think about the philosophical discussions we shared on the banks of the Ganges in India, when a preacher in a church in Singapore says "You are special!"? It is not every day that we go to mass, and it just so happens that we come to this one! This is a sly wink of an eye, and a strong message about the goals that we set for ourselves and the energy that we dedicate to reaching them.

Our encounters seem predestined: without them we wouldn't have been able to live so many unforgettable moments that helped us move forward.

These four days spent in Singapore don't break the rule. As is customary during this journey, we stumble upon gems every day. Firstly, Frances and Paul reach out to us on social media. Since we're stuck in Singapore, we need a place to sleep, and we spend not one, but three nights in their home. Frances, British by birth and living in Singapore for over twenty years, adopts us as if we were her own children. She shows a contagious dynamism, and allows us into her everyday life. Paul, her husband, is a born and raised Singaporean, and he does everything he can to help us out. They both accompany us, they support us, and all without expecting anything in return. These are gestures that, even now, take us by surprise.

Sometimes, though, our morale isn't consistently high. When we leave the rugby match upon which we had placed many of our hopes, we try to raise our spirits by heading to the Marina Bay Sands Hotel. We soon find ourselves on the terraced roof of the hotel, one of those futuristic buildings that Singapore boasts many of. The ambiance here is relaxed, with children playing on one side and friends laughing on the other. The hazy luminosity of the setting sun adds a filter over the scenes that we are witnessing. A little bit farther, sitting at the bar, is a person that attracts our eyes, or at least Muammer's. We share a few words and contact information with J.B. Wood, a distinguished businessman from California, but it is clear that something else is waiting for us...

Anahita. Thanks to her, the dream of arriving in San Francisco has become a reality. Her unexpected message indicating that she will be buying one of the tickets helps to make everything fall into place. Without her, Aziz never would have contacted us all the way from France to sponsor our second ticket. This is an incredible turn of events, and more than that, it is a wonderful encounter. Anahita's presence and her personality, both as luminous as jewels, liven up and enrich our journey. Already, during our first night in Singapore with her husband and son, her dedication had touched us, and as we continue to get to know her, she reveals more about herself: she is cheerful, full of laughter, and of life. Her confessions touch us, and her trust in us make us feel proud. We have made a new friend.

Crazy with joy, we have even more proof now that we mustn't do anything but ride out the storm when bad moments come. Armed with patience, one must always counter negative energies or utilize them to find something better. And here, surrounded by good people, magic operates once more. See you soon, San Francisco!

SOUTH EAST ASIA

57 DAYS = 21 455KM

CHINA

JAPAN

Tokyo

Hong Kong

Bangkok

THAILAND

Chomphon

Koh Tao

Hat Yai

MALAYSIA

Kuala Lumpur

Tangkak

Singapore

Day 57 – Tuesday, November 4th, 2014
Singapore – Hong Kong – Tokyo, Japan – San Francisco, United States

We have barely slept but we already have to head to the airport. Paul drives us, unfazed by the shining 5 AM marked on his dashboard, which is just as well. Our impatience to leave and the prospect of continuing our challenge on another continent don't take long to wake us up fully, and we're soon at the airport.

A long day awaits us: three flights, two layovers, and a fifteen-hour time difference in total. Our conquest of the American West is going to be well-deserved after our long trek! The first plane takes off, leaving Singapore behind us, and a few hours later we arrive in Hong Kong. Taking advantage of the time we have before our next flight, Muammer makes the risky decision of visiting the city, and he experiences a condensed version of Hong Kong for a few hours. He dives into the maze of the glass and steel towers and into the melting-pot of the Chinese city. His encounters there are brief but numerous, and the people he meets are from many countries, with many different personalities. He runs into a Russian top model, an HIV researcher, an English author and composer, and an Australian masseuse, among others. All of these short meetings are enriching, and the personalities he meets, fascinating. This continues in the Tokyo airport, with a 10-year-old Russian athlete and her mother whom we speak to for a while. Every story makes us travel a little bit more.

Third plane, and this time, we leave the Asian continent for good. The Pacific Ocean extends over a vast blue expanse, and at the end, our promised land, San Francisco, is waiting for us. North America, finally. And after, Europe and Paris, very soon. The adventure expands; we have twenty-three days left, everything is possible.

Our friend J.B. Wood picks us up at the airport. We knew very well that our meeting in Singapore was only the beginning of our story together. At the wheel of his blue Jaguar, he savors every moment as he leads us into his world. With a proud and cheerful look, he takes us to Los Gatos, south of the San Francisco Bay. The fatigue of almost 30 hours of flight and the jet lag seem to have no sway over us, or at least we don't feel the symptoms. They are masked by the excitement and the curiosity that this new acquaintance and land bring about.

The dinner that we enjoy that evening immediately thrusts us into the ubiquitous North American culture, and the conversation flows freely and cheerfully. Gina, J.B.'s friend, flutters around the restaurant, assuring the pleasant environment. The contrast between the two continents is satisfying, and the difference, exhilarating. Welcome to California, indeed.

Day 58 – Wednesday, November 5th, 2014
San Francisco, United States

At 6:30 sharp, we are already awake and following the aroma of coffee into the kitchen where Mr. Wood is waiting for us.

He is busy scribbling on a piece of paper: our instructions for the day. Katie, the young waitress that we met last night, is going to show us around San Francisco. On his piece of paper, J.B. has written all manner of suggestions so that we can enjoy our day to the fullest, a kind show of attention.

Unfortunately, Katie has something pop up and cannot come show us around, so J.B. launches Plan B. We no longer need his helpful instructions as he himself will show us around the city! We make our first stop on the shores of the San Francisco Bay. Afterwards, we continue through the obligatory stops of the impressive Golden Gate Bridge, the Palace of Fine Arts, the Ghirardelli Chocolate Factory, all along the avenues, Lombard Street, and Union Square. He pulls out all the stops and San Francisco and its landmarks charm us with ease.

Is it possible to not melt in front of the Victorian-style homes and their colorful architecture, the cable cars, their technology from yesteryear, or the steep and winding streets? The bright sun follows us throughout the day, and the vegetation around the city is wearing its autumnal colors. The sweet California way of life soon wins us over.

J.B. then takes us to his favorite playing ground, where his work and his perseverance have paid off, and where his two companies specializing in new technologies are headquartered: Silicon Valley. Apple, Microsoft, Google, to mention only a few, are some of the iconic names that parade in front of our eyes.

When we return to Los Gatos, we try to map out our adventure. Meeting with passionate and tenacious hard workers like J.B. overjoys us, but we must not rest on our laurels. In terms of our route, we have two choices: the first and quicker one is to go north; the second, to go south. This one takes longer, but the temperature will be more pleasant. We would rather go north, but we decide to go south, after listening to J.B.'s advice. His praise of the California Zephyr, the line that links San Francisco and Chicago, leave us with starry eyes... we will see.

For the moment, J.B. once again plunges us into his festive and warm universe, Surrounded by his friends, he opens up his daily life, even though he barely knew us twenty-four hours ago. We strike up conversations everywhere, and his companions welcome us with open arms. We receive many invitations, and we accept one to test out the Tesla, the latest invention in mobile technology. We experience many strong feelings underneath the moonlit sky; the Silicon Valley makes us dream.

Day 59 – Thursday, November 6th, 2014
San Francisco, United States

North America. California. This journey around the world in eighty days is definitely leading us to beautiful places.

On this fifty-ninth day of the adventure, we wake up in San Francisco, still hosted by J.B. Woods. His generosity and congeniality, qualities that we had already appreciated in Singapore, prove to be decisive in the unfolding of our challenge. Thanks to him, we decide that we are going to cross the United States, from the San Francisco Bay to New York City, not by hitchhiking but by train. He has already bought us one of the tickets, and this allows us to enjoy more time in his company.

We spend a day without thinking about the time, a sort of parenthesis in the frenetic rhythm imposed by our race against the clock. A day where we let ourselves just enjoy all of the benefits of a job well done and the strength of our willpower to get here.

In other words, letting ourselves look at the adventure at a different angle, letting ourselves be surprised by life and the twists of fate that we experience.

Though he is not able to join us due to work-related reasons – being an important businessman leading two companies means that he isn't always free! – our friend prepares another piece of paper full of suggestions for our day and tells us to take his Jaguar, yet another remarkable gesture of trust! Our amazement is off the charts: since the beginning of this adventure, we are constantly going from one world to another.

At the wheel of this swanky car, we head south by taking Highway One along the Pacific Ocean. The rocky coast spreads out at our sides and the splendor of its landscapes is deeply satisfying. Our curiosity gets the best of us and we make several stops; this is an opportunity that we can't miss!

An infinite beach and the ocean stretch before us all the way into the horizon. We feel the sweetness of the sun that pleasantly shines down on us, and we are rocked by the crashing of the waves on the shore. We feel free, and time has come to a standstill. We stay here for what seems to be many hours, time during which we reflect, alone in the face of the immensity, sitting on the beach or walking along the water. Feeling at one with nature, we take advantage of the moment to revitalize our spirits: in a fit of joyful carefreeness, I suggest that we take a dip in the waters of the Pacific Ocean. We don't have bathing suits, but who needs them anyway? Freedom, now and forever!

We are covered in sand but feel reinvigorated when we get back in the car and drive to Carmel, the atypical and touristy small town where villas and sumptuous gardens flow by in succession. We are expected at an inn owned by J.B. Around a platter of cold cuts and cheeses, we discover the spectacular white building. The architecture is magnificent and the vegetation that surrounds it is abundant. Sitting in the shade of some trees in the heart of a patio, close to a fountain, we decide to take several photographs and videos of the place to make a promotional clip to thank our host for his exceptionally warm reception.

The time has come to honor our invitation to J.B.'s friends' home in Los Gatos. Once we're there, Glenn and Karyn Gramling's big wooden house, hanging over the hill, offers an incredible view of the Silicon Valley. Night has fallen, and the city lights are shining as far as the eye can see. The night continues as the day began, rich in surprises and conversations.

Upon arriving at their home, we are touched when we discover around two dozen guests and a cake with a message on it: "Welcome Milan & Muammer". Each person that we talk to is more curious about information and anecdotes from the Optimistic Traveler than the last, and we spend many hours talking about our projects, about ourselves, and about life. Conversations are struck up constantly, and the ambiance in the house is delightful and lively. It is here that we are able to obtain our second train ticket thanks to a totally unexpected collective fundraiser!

Sharing is the word that best characterizes this evening. We feel a strong bond with our host and friend J.B., a father-and-sons relationship, as he calls it. We are incredibly moved by his words. This is a connection that won't be broken, and an encounter that especially touches Muammer, who has lost his father not long ago.

We share a few more moments that night, such as the curiously difficult online purchase of the train tickets for tomorrow – valid for fifteen days and eight stops – and, happy and fulfilled, we go to sleep for a short while.

The anecdotes, the places, and the people that have been gifted to us during this short Californian parenthesis leave us with a mind full of memories and they have touched our spirits with experiences of all kinds.

Day 60 – Friday, November 7th, 2014
San Francisco – Salt Lake City, United States

We went to sleep at 3:30 last night, so it is difficult to wake up two and half hours later. We bid an emotional goodbye to J.B., who drives us to the Gramling's home. Each moment that we spent in his company has moved us immensely and become a source of learning and inspiration.

This departure puts all of our encounters into perspective and gives them a new intensity. When we were planning out our trip, we had expected to work every day to thank our hosts and everyone who gave us a hand, but the generosity of the people we've met along the way has exceeded our expectations. We only hope that our joie de vivre and all of our love that they receive in return is enough to thank them for all their kind gifts.

J.B. looks at us directly in the eyes and tells us: "From now on, I am your father. Before doing anything in life, call me so that I can help you or give you advice."

The life experience and the intelligence of this man have changed a part of us.

The moon disappears and is replaced by the sun, and the valley is bathed in light. We enjoy these magical moments while having breakfast with our friends. Afterwards, and too quickly, the time has come to leave.

Randy, whom we met last night, picks us up as promised to drive us to the train station. We head toward Emeryville, in the north-east of San Francisco, after a pit stop in his house so that he can give us scarfs and hats. We are, after all, heading to the East and into the cold without any sort of equipment...

The small Emeryville train station doesn't look like much, but it is from here that the well-known California Zephyr departs on one of the most beautiful train rides across North America, if the passionate travelers we've met are to be believed.

It is 9 in the morning, and we take our seats on board. The long trip commences: almost 1,400 kilometers separate us from Salt Lake City. Our enthusiasm in the face of this new adventure soon is at its peak, and we curiously get acquainted with our neighbors. We meet a couple who are headed to Reno, in Nevada. Why are they going there, we ask? Oh, to celebrate the lady's 70th birthday, of course! She immediately shows us the itinerary of the festivities, from a cabaret show to a Japanese restaurant and a casino. Farther down, in the adjacent car, soul music is blaring. Upon seeing our surprised expressions, an amused passenger tells us:

"Yeah, DJ on the train!"

Two older ladies quickly add, as if revealing some interesting gossip:

"They used to have one car just for dancing. That was a lot of fun."

Outside, the landscape zooms past. The industrial suburbs are soon replaced by wide open spaces, dense sequoia forests, and lakes. They then turn into plateaus and valleys; the vegetation changes, and the rocky crags cut the horizon.

We continue to converse with the people around us. Some of them share their meals with us, and others bring us bottles of water. We let ourselves be rocked by the nonchalant rhythm of the train, and we soon fall into a deep slumber.

Day 61 – Saturday, November 8th, 2014
Salt Lake City, United States

We open our eyes just in time to get off at the Salt Lake City platform. It is 3:30 in the morning, pitch dark, and freezing, especially compared to the temperatures that we have been living in for the last couple of months. We take one look at each other and we tacitly agree that if we don't want to spend the night outside, the time to act is now. It all plays out over a few minutes where we speak to the handful of people that got out with us, but success is not on the program for today. We set off, resigned to our fate, toward the downtown area.

We spend two long hours, freezing and numb, wandering the empty streets of the city without a clear objective. We are lucky to be able to warm up in front of a blazing fireplace in the lobby of a hotel before setting out again. As we walk, we re-center. At this hour, the city is still sleeping, and only homeless people are wandering the streets. We talk with one of them about the aid they receive, and about the way shelters work in the city. Sporting a black eye, he confesses to us that yes, one effectively has to watch out for himself and for his things. Our previous complaints seem insignificant all of a sudden...

The sun has finally risen, and the early birds are all beginning their days. Our next encounter reminds us of another difference in this culture that is still foreign to us: Salt Lake City is the worldwide seat of the Mormon religion, or the Church of the Latter-Day Saints. Ralph, aged 77 and a father of seven, tells us his story and points us in the direction of the Temple Square, a site that gathers the house of worship, the administrative buildings of the Church, the conference center, the museum, and the library. We spend a portion of our morning trying to learn more about this religion through taking tours guided by missionary nuns.

The rest of the day leads us across the city and allows us to continue meeting people. From an out-of-the-ordinary barber shop we head toward the outskirts of Salt Lake City to visit a Mormon mission, where Scott, the manager, offers us two jackets. Our comings and goings onboard the public buses place us in the path of several people, and it is with two foreign students that we head toward the university campus. From there, after a quintessential American peanut butter and jelly sandwich, we follow a hiking path that leads us to a spot overlooking the city and offers up a magnificent vista. This hike has done us a world of good, and we enjoy the view. The colors of the sky during the sunset are hypnotizing, and we profit from this moment of symbiosis with nature before descending toward the center of the city where things are hopping.

It is a game night in Salt Lake City, where football is certainly not taken lightly. The supporters have invaded the streets, and the ambiance is impressive.

On this festive note, we take advantage of our last hours in Salt Lake City in the company of Shanay, Stacey, and their friends, whom we met earlier on the mountain, far away from this tumultuous scene.

Day 62 – Sunday, November 9th, 2014
Salt Lake City – Denver, United States

At 3:30 in the morning, we once again board the California Zephyr to go to our next stop, Denver. The car is completely dark and silence reigns over the space. The passengers are all sleeping, and once we take our seats, we try to do the same.

A few hours later, we wake up under bright skies. The morning light makes every color sublime; the red of the rocks and the cliffs, the ochre of the canyons we pass by, the golden tones of the flora dressed for autumn, and the glacial blue of the sky and the Colorado River that flows by our sides. The grandiose landscapes of the American West accompany our daydreams and our fantasies. The Rockies are certainly worthy of all fascination.

The cadence of the train creates a peculiar sensation, a sort of rhythm, a time and space of its own. We glide in this enclosed space toward another dimension, and feel completely submerged in the universe of the California Zephyr.

We explore every nook and cranny of this new universe, from the tight hallways to the panoramic car filled with Amish families and their hordes of children. Each one is lost in their own world, but they still offer kind smiles to their travel companions, just like the personnel of the Amtrak line that are milling around.

Later, as is our custom in places like these, we strike up several conversations and let ourselves be surprised by the people we meet. Quickly, a francophone team is formed with two voyagers who are traveling alone, heading to Chicago: Nicolas, first, and then Gaëlle, who observes more than she participates in the exchanges. We are intrigued by her quiet demeanor, and she soon explains it to us. She is reserved, sure, but she also expresses herself better through writing. We insist that she show us some of her writing, and as we read her words, we feel touched by her art. Naturally, we soon start thinking of how we can collaborate with her one day, and only time can tell what will come of this new relationship...

The light outside changes colors, and the day fades away. Denver is in front of us, not too far. The trip continues as we spread our good moods and excitement to the passengers that surround us. Many conversations are still going on, here and there. Milan chats briefly with an American couple, Steve and Debra, who later come to tell us that one of their friends will be able to host us tonight. This is news that overjoys and reassures us, of course.

We enjoy the brilliantly-colored sunset before we are once more plunged into darkness, leaving our parallel world to step into reality: Denver, Colorado. We follow Steve and Debra into the station, and are then joined by their son. Together, we head to our host's address, where Panayoti opens the doors to his home with a simplicity and warmth that marvel us. We drop off our bags with the impression that a beautiful story is about to begin.

Day 63 – Monday, November 10th, 2014
Denver, United States

Panayoti, or P.K. as he's nicknamed, is an absolutely passionate and welcoming man. With his partner, he receives us as if we were old friends or even his own children. A curator and the director of research and development of the botanical garden in Denver, he has traveled all over the world and seeks out foreign cultures when he has conferences abroad. His skills and wisdom, as well as his humor, are a great inspiration to us.

We have met many people since we left Paris. Every one of them has had interesting and unique stories, and some of them have touched us tremendously. P.K.'s presence and the time that he devotes to our cause are an honor for us. Not satisfied with simply opening the doors of his personal life, he invites

162

us to discover his professional world, as well. We discover the paths and the secrets of the botanical garden and we understand, thanks to his words, the reasons that drew him to be involved in this field:

"As forests and fields are vastly reduced, botanical gardens become the places where nature takes back its rights in the hearts of cities. They act as reminders so that we don't forget how important plants are to humans, especially in the field of medicine."

Our peculiar way of traveling has often offered us the opportunity to get to know different points of view on many things, and this is just another. We are humbled to have the opportunity to become conscious of the world that surrounds us and of the people that populate it.

We spend our first morning in Denver at the botanical garden in the company of our host, and then we leave to explore the center of the city in the afternoon flow. The last rays of sunlight are shining down, and soon disappear. The sunny days of seasons past are now behind us as winter takes hold of Colorado.

Snowflakes flutter around us and the icy gusts of wind freeze us to the bone. We have a hard time dealing with the negative temperatures and our resistance is quickly beaten. This is very much like when, in Salt Lake City, reality caught up with us in the middle of the street. The homeless people in Denver withstand the cold for lack of any other choice. These difficult scenes of their everyday life leave us with a desire to be able to help - bringing aid to people in need, here or there, during the course of this challenge and beyond, is one of our dearest desires.

Tired but, now more optimistic than ever in the face of our mission, we reunite with Panayoti. Back at his house, we help his wife to prepare dinner in the kitchen. Steve and Debra come over for the evening, and the good mood and companionship in the house are beautiful to witness. When she arrives, Debra can't hide her excitement: earlier in the day, she called her church to be able to gather coats for our trip north, and she holds out a bag full of the garments. We have nothing left to do but to choose which ones we want and to thank her profusely for her kind gesture. Afterwards, between jokes, anecdotes, and a lovely meal, we savor this evening. Once our guests have left and the lights have been turned out, it doesn't take us long to fall into a deep sleep.

Day 64 – Tuesday, November 11th, 2014
Denver – Chicago, United States

It is our second morning in Panayoti's house, and we have no time to waste today. After eating breakfast in this now familiar environment, we gather our things and go to the botanical garden, where we are expected. To our great surprise, a reunion has been planned around the theme of Optimistic Traveler, to which all of P.K.'s colleagues and the director of the garden are invited.

We talk for several hours about the challenge that has set the rhythm of our days since September 9th, and take special care to place importance on the messages of humanity that we have witnessed, know that must share and spread them in exchange. After this enriching reflection, P.K. remarks:

"Well, as we can see this wasn't just a normal personnel meeting."

Winter has relentlessly taken root in Denver. A fine layer of snow covers the city and the thermometers are all negative. In this environment, we leave our new friend P.K. with heavy hearts, and meet Mike for a meal. Our adventure has fascinated and inspired this young student ever since he heard about it, and when his mother, who was present for our meeting at the botanical garden, called him and proposed that he join us, he jumped at the occasion. His ambition, once he finishes his degree, is to travel the world to volunteer and our challenge reassures him that this is a good choice.

He also tells us his complicated relationship with his stepfather and his inexistent one with his biological father, and about his doubts in the matter. One thing leads to another and we arrive at an interesting proposition: to help him clear his head, we will help him to clean his car. We have never seen such a dirty vehicle! There are knickknacks everywhere, and trash invades the space. We spend more than an hour organizing, throwing away trash, cleaning, and vacuuming the vehicle. This is an efficient way to clear one's head, and a lovely way to spend time together.

The moment has come to return to the train station, but we have some free time as the train doesn't leave until the end of the day. The Terminal Café and its employees greet us with enthusiasm, and Alyssa offers us drinks and a meal, while her friend Josh does everything he can to make sure that the news of our arrival in Chicago spreads through the social media sites. We might be able to find lodging thanks to this generous initiative!

Later on, close to the platforms, we meet Jake. He is only 21, but he has been living for two years in the street. He has no job, and unfortunately can't be supported by his sister who doesn't have enough means to take care of him. A new opportunity is presented to him today in the form of a train ticket to join his mother in Milwaukee.

We are suddenly interrupted by the surprise arrival of Stefany, P.K.'s neighbor. She bursts into the station hall and she comes to say goodbye to us. She has taken it upon herself to create a sort of survival kit for each of us, and she leaves as quickly as she arrived. In each kit, we find tissues, antibacterial gel, an insulated mug, a scarf, a beanie, and mittens; she has thought of everything! There is more than enough for the two of us, and we share the thoughtful gift with Jake, who is happy to receive some of these useful items.

The train has arrived at the station, and the passengers head to the platform. Melissa catches our eye immediately; with her purple hair, her piercings, and her expertly-drawn eyeliner, she doesn't pass by unnoticed. Paradoxically, her bold style belies a fragile sweetness. She stands before us, like a porcelain doll with freezing hands, and following the advice of a friend who has driven her to the station, we decide to travel in her company and make sure that she is all right during the trip.

We take our seats on the California Zephyr that we're beginning to be familiar with. We rediscover its cadence and its particular tune, and between reading, discussions, and work, we head east along the dark night.

Day 65 – Wednesday, November 12th, 2014
En route to Chicago, United States

The people we meet in the parallel universe of the California Zephyr are all unique. On this morning of November 12th, we wake up feeling deeply moved. Melissa has left us a letter before getting off the train. In it she tells us of her distress and suffering. She confesses that meeting Optimistic Traveler has shaken her up and given her hope once more. She has found new faith in humanity and decides to give life a new chance.

The emotion that we feel is immense, and tears moisten our eyes. What if the purpose of this journey, of this challenge, was to cross her path, and save her? We aren't experts in the law of life, but in a moment like this we feel obligated to believe in destiny and in the magic of spiritual energy.

We are troubled, but we make an effort to continue forward, and the diversity and quality of our next encounters replenishes our spirits.

Muammer speaks for a long time with Jake, whom he has found on the train, while I leave to explore the panoramic car.

The stories are all different. One woman is traveling to attend her brother's wedding while another, Jessica, has just left everything behind to live out her dream in New York City. Looks are exchanged, and relationships are formed. As the hours go by, we see the same people and indifference is no longer present on the train. Outside, the plains of Illinois succeed those of Iowa and the cities that zoom by all present their industrial side to us.

The arrival of Andrew determines the direction that we head in next. A graphic designer and musician in his free time, he lives in the suburbs of Chicago with his roommates. The doors of his home are always open, and visitors are always welcome. He doesn't hesitate before proposing that we stay there, and his good humor and warmth accompany us during the last hours of the train ride.

Finally, we arrive in Chicago, Illinois. Our arrival in the city marks the beginning of a very interesting night. Gaëlle and

Nicolas, the two French people we met on the California Zephyr between Salt Lake City and Denver, surprise us at the train station. Seeing two familiar faces in the crowd is not normal for us during this journey, and we greet them happily. These are reunions that we must celebrate!

We head to a bar at Union Station, and Jessica joins us before catching her connection. The live music is thumping, and the ambiance is delightful. We talk about our respective pilgrimages, and the smiles and laughter are soothing to our hearts. Jessica soon must leave to catch her train, and we consider that the time spent with our friends has been too short, so we bring them with us to Andrew's place!

The taxi ride to get to the west part of the city is a memorable one. In a city with 8,000 taxis, the chances of stumbling upon the same one twice are slim, but this doesn't stop Gaëlle from instantly recognizing the driver that had driven her around just two days earlier. We don't need any more of an excuse to commence a conversation with him. He is Moroccan, and he speaks to us in French about his country that he misses so much.

Soon, we arrive at Andrew's house. Nicole, his girlfriend, opens the doors to the aptly-named Louder House. Against all expectations, and like on the California Zephyr, we feel like we're entering a new dimension. The house's inhabitants are brimming with creative energy, and the decoration all around is attractive and fascinating, like a cabinet of curiosities. Music is omnipresent here, as well as positive vibes. Two cats, one black and one white, two chickens, and a turtle are also residents of this amazing dwelling. Joe, Zack, and then Adam join us for a bonfire in the backyard. Something between a rite and good-natured fun, we let ourselves be carried away by this sweet folly. The evening continues in the basement, which has been turned into a painting and filming studio. Andrew, Joe, and Zack kick us off, and soon we're off on an hours-long journey of musical improvisation. At first we were astounded yet content just watching, but we soon take part in this joyful bazaar. Destiny has put us in the path of fascinating characters, passionate people who wear their heart on their sleeves.

It's getting late, or early, no one knows. Nicolas and Gaëlle return to the places where they're staying, and we, tired but blissful, are more than happy to have been able to live and share this unforgettable evening in their company.

Day 66 – Thursday, November 13th, 2014
Chicago, United States

We sleep in this morning at the Louder House, trying to recover some of the hours of rest that we lost last night. Little by little, the roommates of the house emerge and tend to their business. Joe joins us in the living room, and around a coffee, the conversation soon takes a deeper and more serious tone. While talking about our projects, specifically Haiti Care, he shares with us his father's efforts to bring education to needy children, a remarkable initiative.

After a bike ride around the neighborhood with Andrew, we leave with Joe in the direction of Wicker Park, an up-and-coming arts quarter in the west area of Chicago. A muralist and rising artist, Joe Miller is a surprising man. As soon as we arrive, he abandons his studio to dedicate himself fully to us. Today, it is inconceivable to him to not show us around his city.

His life story is captivating and we try to learn more about the details, such as his bicycle journey across the United States. He confesses that he didn't learn much from this experience in terms of lessons, but he did become conscious of the values that he had been taught up until that moment and that he wanted to present every day. Patience, humility, sharing, compassion, and open-mindedness have been his guiding lights since then.

We are now in the Loop, the downtown of Chicago. The wind has chased away the clouds and the snowflakes, leaving behind a bright blue sky. The city is majestic in the glacial cold, and the iconic North American architecture transports us immediately. The skyscrapers are imposing, the facades of theatres glitter with their neon signs, and wisps of steam float out of grates in the streets. The Chicago of Al Capone and the Blues legends isn't far from here...

The day continues with our encounter with Hami, a director from Madagascar. We can see that art is the central thread that connects all of our adventures in the Windy City so far. Our time with Hami becomes a family reunion as his young son, his wife, and his mother soon join us. We profit from a private screening of his documentary, Legend of Madagascar, a road movie that shows the difficulties that young Malagasy people face in that country. This is, once again, an opportunity to learn about varied and fascinating subjects.

We then find ourselves at a party thrown by Joe's friends in a bar in the northwest of Chicago. The place is incredible, a complex including a hotel, a spa, a gym, a restaurant, and a bar, all housed within a rehabilitated warehouse dating back to the beginning of the Twentieth Century.

It is getting late, so we decide to hitch a ride back home and initiate Joe into our way of traveling. Once again, we meet someone completely unexpected: a young Venezuelan opera singer picks us up without hesitating for a second. Her faith in a better life and her devotion to her work are impressive, and we admire her very much. On the last notes of an Ave Maria, we conclude this magnificent sixty-sixth day of the adventure.

Day 67 – Friday, November 14th, 2014
Chicago, United States

Our stay in Chicago is extended and we experience a new facet to our challenge: it is effectively the first time that we choose to stay for such a long time in one place, as we evidently aren't ready to leave the Louder House and its occupants.

We don't leave the house the entire day but inactivity is not on today's program. In an attempt to be useful and looking for any way to show our gratitude for the hospitality we have received, we offer our assistance in any task that may come up. Inspired by this idea, the "sweet impact" as Joe calls it, the housemates decide to, with our help, tackle the renovation of a room in the basement that had previously served as a storage space.

Encouraged by our good moods and the music playing in the background, we attack the seemingly unending mountain of boxes, crates, furniture, and other odds and ends left there over the course of many years. Once the walls are sanded and painted, and the shelves and the desk are organized, the new painting studio is almost complete. The addition of candles, a string of lights, and a hanging banner is the final touch, and we finish just in time for the beginning of Nicole's birthday festivities.

With the guests crowding in the living room, we serve the dinner prepared by Andrew and the queen of the party soon makes her entrance. It is an enchanting evening of music, dance, and a bonfire; the appreciated charm of proceedings is out in force. A pleasant surprise completes this already enjoyable day: Stéphanie, who has been following our adventure on the internet since the beginning, arrives with her friends after a seven-hour flight! The party is even more fun now, and it continues until the middle of the night.

And us? Well, in terms of this stage of our journey, our bond with Andrew and Joe fills us with happiness and we are pleased to live to the beat of this incredible household.

Day 68 – Saturday, November 15th, 2014
Chicago – Washington, D.C., United States

In this adventure, there are some days where, regardless of our overall plans, our activities aren't so clear-cut, and we let ourselves be carried along by the events of the day instead of setting them up ourselves. This November Saturday is one of those days.

It begins rather slowly in the wake of last night's party. After shopping for some groceries, we assemble in the living room. Between the housemates and the survivors of the soirée, there are at least a dozen people around the breakfast table, all taking their time to wake up. The ambiance is calm, with the soft rays of sunlight streaming in through the windows. We appreciate the moment, surrounded by our hosts and their friends.

We can't hold back our emotions when the time comes to leave. The road is calling us, even though we feel like we're leaving behind a new family. We thank Andrew who, with an amused look, offers us a book called A Man without a Country, and his sly wink makes us smile. Our story with Joe, however, isn't yet finished, since he has decided that he will join us in some months in the Haiti Care project. We are already impatient to once again have him with us. We reach Chicago's train station by car. A last goodbye and a shrill train whistle mark our departure.

Day 69 – Sunday, November 16th, 2014
En route to Washington, D.C., United States

It is still surprising and disconcerting to see how a journey can change one's perceptions. The loss of reference points, a diminished rapport with others, and communication difficulties are just some of the disruptions that we react to using our sensibilities.

During the train ride to Washington, D.C., we pass the time by amusedly pointing out just how much our notion of time has become distorted. Living in a world where we are very often stressed out and pressed by time, it was unthinkable to us just a few months ago that it could also be so elastic.

Twenty-four hours cooped up in a train creates a black night, and a morose day. Outside of our window, the landscapes zoom by, unchanging, kilometer after kilometer. We could, like the majority of the passengers, manifest our impatience and our annoyance at the slow pace of the voyage, but we don't. Instead, our accumulated fatigue and our general lack of energy make us content to let ourselves be rocked in this comfortable and relatively calm environment.

Hunger soon rears its head, though, and makes us come out of this stupor sooner than expected. The few cereal bars collected here and there don't satisfy us and we are soon dreaming of a hot meal. It's thanks to the ticket inspector that we find our salvation: within seconds of hearing about our adventure, he is leading us to the restaurant car to offer us something to eat. A few mouthfuls of sandwich perk us up in no time and, a little bit later, another of the Amtrak employees slides us over four surprise boxes containing compotes, cookies, and other treats. Already satisfied, we share these with the people around us.

Now, with our strength replenished and well into the day, we take up the task of searching for a place to stay for the night. The occasional discussions that emerge from our exchanges are pleasant, but the flame just isn't there. Given this situation, we decide to switch gears: in turns, in each car, we try to appeal to people's minds by means of a speech where we quickly present our mission. We don't elicit many reactions, but we only need one for our fortunes to turn.

In this way we find ourselves in the company of Catarina on the platform of the Alexandria train station, south of Washington, D.C., at the beginning of the evening. An anthropologist and ethnologist, she immediately identifies with us and offers us a hand. Vivian, her friend, is waiting for us a short distance away. She takes us to her home, a small, American-style house situated in a residential neighborhood, where we meet her husband, Dan. We spend an enjoyable evening having dinner and talking about childhood memories and travels, and, after an initial hesitation, Vivian and Dan invite us to spend the night in their basement guest room.

Lost in our thoughts, we reflect on the path we have taken from the west coast of the United States. No more than ten days to reach Paris!

Day 70 – Monday, November 17th, 2014
Washington, D.C., United States

Upon waking, we are greeted by cereal, coffee, and The Washington Post on the kitchen table. Vivian, always attentive to us, has also left us a message accompanied by metro cards and a map of the city. Finally ready, we leave our place to crash in Alexandria, packs on our backs. Dan drives us to the metro station and rides with us for part of the trip. We pass by the Pentagon and it is a little difficult to realize that it is the actual headquarters of the United States Department of Defense and not just a replica on a film set. Afterward, we arrive in downtown D.C.

The torrential rain accompanies us throughout the whole day, and we contemplate spending the hours devoted to the cultural aspects of the city – indoors. The free admission to several different museums convinces us, and we take our time discovering the historical and artistic treasures that D.C. is brimming with, from the Smithsonian National Air and Space Museum to the National Gallery of Art, from the Obelisk to the Capitol, passing by the White House. Patricia, a young Mexican woman and aspiring pilot, gives us the pleasure of joining us for the majority of our pilgrimages in the city and the opportunity to share this experience and to see, in a certain way, these landmarks through her eyes.

Our friend Joe from Chicago puts us in contact with two of his friends who live in Washington, and we go to their apartment at the end of the day. Samantha, her face lit up with a smile, greets us. Her enthusiasm and kindness are constant through the night. Brady, her husband, arrives a little bit later. Around a meal of banana pancakes, boiled eggs, and bacon – a breakfast for dinner, according to Samantha – they tell us about their recent engagement and wedding with stars in their eyes. Their happiness is contagious!

Once we are lying down with our eyes closed, we relive the different stages of our journey that parade in our memories, and the thousands of images we have collected echo in our minds. Reaching Washington was no small feat, given that we crossed an entire new continent. The challenge progresses, as does our path, and these lines from George Washington that we read during the course of our day illustrate our thoughts:

"My first wish is to see the whole world in peace, and its inhabitants one band of brothers striving who should contribute most to the happiness of mankind[15]."

Day 71 – Tuesday, November 18th, 2014
Washington, D.C. – Philadelphia, United States

The call of our challenge sounds like a siren today. Even though our train tickets, which are still valid, allow us to easily continue the route to New York City, we decide to hitchhike to The City on the highway. We warmly thank our hosts and,

following Brady's instructions, take the metro to reach the outskirts of the city.

A magnificent sun has replaced last night's rainy skies. There is no more humidity in the air, but we feel the cold of the day. Luckily for us, we quickly catch Alex's eye. From the other side of the street, he calls out to us and turns around to pick us up. Originally from New York but living in D.C., he drives us along for a distance and drops us off right on the edge of the highway. Alex, with his cap firmly perched on his head and a bandana tied around his neck, plunges us into the "gangsta" universe. Speaking with words that occasionally confuse us but that deeply move us, he tells us of his past as a convict and the lessons that he learned from that time. He then subtly brings his words to our project, which he finds fascinating.

---

15   George Washington, letter to the Marquis of Cleverness,
      7 October 1785.

"The mentality and the attitude with which we face life, that is what allows us to move forward. Unfortunately, it is often fear and pride that guide our path."

Something to think about.

Our trip continues at a brisk pace thanks to Alpha, with whom we ride for almost an hour. It is only when he drops us off at a rest stop next to the highway that things darken a little. Even though crowds are plenty around restaurants and cafés, approaching them is difficult. Due to a lack of time, or fear, or simply because they don't want to help, the people rush past, closed to our efforts. As always, a few are ready to give us money, which we refuse, and others share meals with us, but the negative responses punctuated with aggressive phrases such as "Go away!", "Leave me alone!", and "Never in my life!" abound when we ask for a ride.

After a long while, our encounter with Tim puts us back on track. In his beautiful car, we finally advance toward Philadelphia. Our positive interaction with this young entrepreneur revives our energy, which had been on the verge of dying out, and since the afternoon is well past, we find it prudent to accept his proposition of staying at his home in Philadelphia for the night. Tim immediately cancels his plans for the night in order to host us, something that has never happened to us before!

The historic buildings and the glass towers in the downtown of the city greet us in all of their contrasting and imperial glory. We drop off our backpacks at Tim's brother's apartment, not far from downtown, and we set off to salute the legendary statue of Rocky Balboa, a mandatory visit, as is the climb up the famous steps of the Philadelphia Museum of Art. After this short parenthesis, we take advantage of the waning light of day to discover Philly under a new light.

We make a short return to the apartment for a perilous make-over. Tim transforms our appearance by dressing us up in suits, the required dress code, before taking us to The Union League of Philadelphia, a prestigious club. Looking like real gentlemen, we slowly glide around this mind-boggling universe. We navigate the halls of this historical building, hypnotized by the objects we see, each more noble than the last: furniture made out of the most burnished of woods, marble floors, leather couches, chandeliers, stained-glass windows, paintings, and ornaments. Together, they make for an incredible picture. Wisps of cigar smoke that escape from the multiple lounges add a light filter to the décor. The atmosphere that emanates from the place and the fantasy that it evokes bewitches us.

Tonight, far away from the fundamental ideas of our adventure, we delightedly observe the magnificent scenes that we are privy to thanks to the encounters that we have made along the route.

Day 72 – Wednesday, November 19th, 2014
Philadelphia – New York City, United States

We don't delay our departure this morning. A quick shower and an espresso after waking up is all we need, and then the three of us are on the sidewalk. The weather is radiant: cold, but sunny. Along the way we pick up a bite to eat at a café next to the parking lot. Once we're in the car, we're carried away by the morning traffic flow. Philadelphia soon fades away behind us as Tim drives us out of the city for about an hour, a godsend because we know firsthand just how difficult it is to hitchhike out of big cities.

We leave our new friend and we begin to flag down cars close to the exit that leads to the northbound Interstate 95. Vehicles drive by regularly, but none of them stop for us. The freezing temperature is hard to support for long and we quickly take refuge in a nearby diner.

We study our possibilities. We are currently in Levittown, a town with a name that isn't completely foreign to us, and for good reason: a few days ago, we received a message from a Turkish family that resides here. They have been following our adventures on social media sites, and they wish to meet us. We get in touch with them, not knowing what will come of this decision, and soon we are waiting for the wife to come pick us up.

Imagine Muammer's surprise when he sees his cousin, whom he has not seen in the last twenty years, enter the restaurant! The physical distance, the adventure, and the rather large family tree of their grandfather (which includes more than 250 living relatives!) have all come in between these two cousins, who haven't been able to talk much outside of written exchanges. Encounters like these don't happen often, so we decide to spend several emotion-filled moments with the family before setting off again. After riding with them on the interstate toward New York City and sharing a warm meal in their company, they drop us off in Times Square.

A few kisses later, we dive right back into the challenge. We spend three hours there, asking people outside theatres and restaurants and at a subway station, trying to find a host for the night. The reactions we face are often closed and final, and we run into several French tourists who, unfortunately, cannot do anything to help us. Even though we're happy to be in New York City, a place that is familiar to us, our hopes ebb away with each passing minute, and the fatigue and the cold aren't helping. Late that night, defeated, we decide to get in touch with Tamer, Muammer's cousin, and he picks us up in no time.

It's official: we broke the rules that we had fixed for this adventure. It is obvious to us now that even a place that we find familiar can play tricks on us, but it is important to be able to go with the flow and not control everything.

Day 73 – Thursday, November 20th, 2014
New York City, United States

New York City. Manhattan. The Empire State Building, the yellow taxis, the large avenues... The City. Its positive energy and dynamic environment are at the heart of this day filled with new encounters and experiences.

Our excitement drives us out of our beds this morning. We rapidly get to know the roommates of Tamer and Rebecca, his Brazilian fiancée. Their stories, confidences that we love hearing, are familiar to our ears: a taste for the challenge and the multiple possibilities of this city have brought them all to New York to pursue their studies.

This same taste for the challenge calls out to us today. During the bus ride that leads us to Manhattan, we can't hide our smiles. On this sunny afternoon, we are meeting with Sibylle at the UN. Living for more than ten years in New York City, she is currently an international functionary in the Counter-Terrorism Committee at the United Nations, and is also a children's book author. Thanks to Sibylle, the doors of this organization are open to us and, once we pass through the security checkpoint, we begin our visit. The surrealism of the situation is deeply moving: after crossing three continents thanks to the sheer goodwill and humanity of people and arriving in New York City, the seat of the United Nations, the symbolism is strong and our hope is immense.

Émeline, a journalist at French Morning, an online magazine for French-speakers living in the United States, joins us later, taking notes for an article she is writing about us. We share a meal with her and talk for hours while enjoying a magnificent view of the Chrysler Tower. Sibylle tells us about her epic trip to New York on a cargo ship a few years earlier and her well-filled schedule. Émeline then shares stories about trips she's taken similar to our Optimistic Traveler challenge. When she was younger, she went across France with her brother and shook up her habits by going and knocking on people's doors to find places to stay. These are the kinds of experiences that guarantee memories.

Our paths diverge for a few hours before we meet again, not far from the UN, at the World Bar for the "Beaujolais Nouveau" party, of which we are the guests of honor. The francophone community of New York City and several functionaries of the UN are present, and we rejoice at having this opportunity to find a receptive audience and to share our message. We are one step closer to the realization of our ambitions

Our day ends in the company of Kenneth, the owner of the bar, with whom we had a congenial conversation. He invites us to stay at his place and, once we drop off our backpacks at his apartment, we go with him to meet with some of his friends. The city nightlife fascinates us and we enjoy it as much as we can, until we can fight the fatigue no longer and decide to go home to sleep.

Day 74 – Friday, November 21st, 2014
New York City, United States

We wake up in the heart of Manhattan, in Kenneth's apartment, happy in the knowledge that even now, close to the end of this adventure, we are still pleasantly surprised by the hospitality and the kindness of our hosts.

The dynamic owner of eight establishments, Kenneth takes us to one of his cafés, a few blocks away from his place, to have breakfast. He can't stay with us for long, so he speaks with his employees before leaving us. On his recommendation, they pamper us and serve us a meal fit for a king.

Afterwards, we make our way back to the UN where we are meeting with Dorian, whom we met last night at the party. This time, the doors of the General Assembly are opened for us, as well as those of the mythical Security Council Chamber. We are covered in goosebumps, and how could we not when we are discovering these places full of meaning and history? The cherry on the top happens when Dorian mentions us at the daily press conference, an honor and a distinction for Optimistic Traveler.

With stars in our eyes, we meet Reina, whom we met briefly during our layover in the Tokyo Airport two weeks earlier. Since we're in New York City at the same time, it was inconceivable to not see her again. Her sweet nature and her smile accompany us during the last hours we spend in New York. Dizzy with joy, we celebrate our reunion around a meal, and then we head to a café.

There, we have yet another incredible encounter. Gerardo, the young manager of the café, joins us immediately after he finds out about our challenge, and he generously offers us complimentary drinks and pastries. However, it is his speech most of all that we keep with us. We listen, fascinated, to him speak about his vision of the world and of humanity. Incredibly elegant in his blue pinstriped suit accessorized with a pocket handkerchief, his hair slicked back, Gerardo deeply moves us with his words. It is with a smile that briefly escapes from his lips that he shares his hopeful cry:

"You have to give yourself a chance. I have problems, you have problems, but we have to allow ourselves to be happy. Learning to live with what you do have will lead to happiness."

His words are surprisingly profound for a man of his age. Reina has tears in her eyes, and we won't be forgetting this moment anytime soon; once again, we are reminded of the magic of this adventure. This is a marvelous conclusion to our chapter in the United States.

The time has come to head toward the JFK airport. Night has fallen, and we take one last look at the city that never sleeps. Its twinkling lights shine as if they were encouraging us.

We are flying to Marrakesh tonight. We decided on this itinerary by chance, given the opportunities given to us by our sponsors, and we are very satisfied with the outcome. Unlike in Singapore, we didn't have trouble finding plane tickets; once we secured the ones to cross the Pacific Ocean, propositions kept coming in. Since we didn't want to be turned away upon our arrival in the United States, we needed to have tickets assuring our departure from the country. The people that we came in contact with on the internet generously proposed to help us with tickets allowing us to return to Europe. Thus, a friend of Jana, the Czech guide that we met in India, and Christiane, a French woman, give us the opportunity to go the end of our challenge.

It is up to us, then, to not disappoint the people that are supporting us during these last days that we have left.

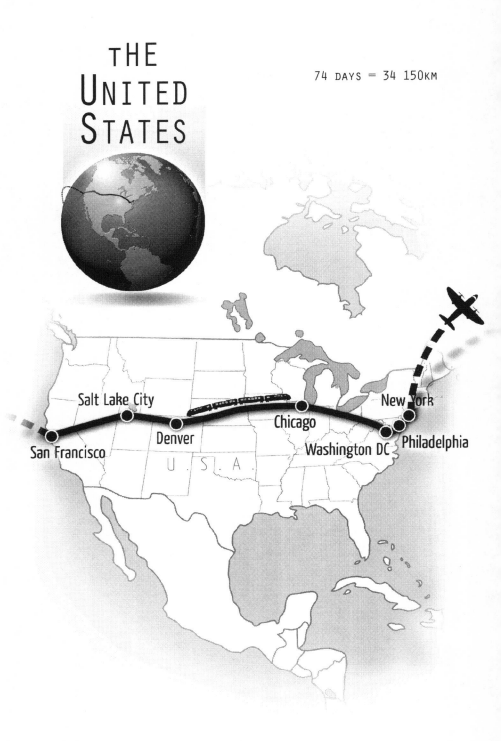

tHE
UNITED
STATES

74 DAYS = 34 150KM

Salt Lake City

Denver

Chicago

New York

Washington DC

Philadelphia

San Francisco

U.S.A.

Day 75 – Saturday, November 22nd, 2014
New York City, United States – Oslo, Norway – Marrakesh, Morocco

After two flights and a short layover in Oslo, Norway, we take our first steps on Moroccan soil. We are in Africa, yet another continent, and in another culture, with many encounters yet to come. We are delighted, day after day, to enjoy the opportunities that this journey around the world has offered us.

We are in the Marrakesh airport, brimming with excitement at the idea of conquering Northern Africa, the last stage before the grand finale. We head to the bus parked outside and we speak with the driver. Barely after asking, he graciously allows us on board; the Moroccan hospitality scores points!

Gérard, a witness of the scene, is amazed by it. We sit next to him during the ride downtown, and we share our respective projects. A Belgian man, Gérard has recently moved to Marrakesh to enjoy his retirement, and we have barely asked the question when he proposes that we stay at his place for the night; The Belgian-Moroccan hospitality scores points!

After arriving at the Jemaa el-Fna square in the center of the city, we get off the bus and agree to meet Gérard later that night. Right now, an exploration of the city is on the menu. The place is buzzing with people, and horse-drawn carriages circle around everywhere. The beat of percussion instruments adds a certain rhythm to the scene, and the effervescence is contagious. From a souk surrounded by vegetation-filled terraces, we marvel at the sights around us. All of our senses are at attention, stimulated. We are once again encircled by the Middle-Eastern culture, intense and dream-like.

In the labyrinth of commercial and artisan shops, we meet Abdoul, who invites us to eat in his restaurant. We enjoy a meal of grilled meats, vegetables, and couscous, which is made all the more satisfying due to the fact that we haven't eaten for hours. Afterwards, in another spot in the marketplace, Diane's smile attracts us. The manager of the El Alhambra café, she offers us tea and pastries, as well as her time and her charming company.

After this, as if we hadn't already experienced plenty of generosity, Ayoub ushers us into his taxi and drives us to our meeting place with Gérard, who is already there waiting for us. We go to his apartment, and talk for a long time about his journeys, his friends, his life, and we discover the secrets of a perfectly executed Moroccan mint tea, a skill that he graciously shares with us. Afterwards, the exhaustion from the travel and the jetlag makes our eyelids droop, and we happily slide into our beds.

Day 76 – Sunday, November 23rd, 2014
Marrakesh – Tangier, Morocco

First morning in Morocco, and the initial thing we do is take a peek out the window. There is no doubt about it, we are definitely on a different continent. The brown earthen homes have taken the place of the New York skyscrapers, and the Atlas Mountains are our new skyline.

Our goal for the day is to reach Tangier, in the northern section of the country. 600 kilometers separate us from that city, and we'll be able to take advantage of the opportunity to test our hitchhiking skills in a new playing field. It is 8 in the morning, and Gérard buys us a crepe and some tea in a café that is just opening before showing us where we should go.

Posted on the side of the road, we pick up our old habits. While waving our hands, making big gestures, jumping, sprinting toward the cars that stop, and making a quick introductory speeches, we can see that our skills are expertly honed and inexhaustible... and they pay off! Still, we owe our success to the people that stop for us; if we reach our goal and we are able to set down our backpacks in Tangier tonight, Sunday, it is entirely thanks to those that accept us in their vehicles. Once again, we are experiencing a stage in our journey that puts us in touch with moving and welcoming individuals.

As always, the hitchhiking experience is punctuated by refusals and long waits, but we nonetheless advance bit by bit. Abdelatif is the first to pick us up and takes us to a service station in the outskirts of Marrakesh. Afterwards, Saïda takes a detour to drive us to the tollgate, all while good-naturedly telling us about her latest anecdotes and her passion for the marathon. We spend an energizing part of the trip in her company.

We then join a family on their way to Casablanca. Mohammed, Nahima, and their three daughters, aged 3 to 12 years old, Assia, Hafsa, and Kawtar are our company on this next part of the trip, and the spontaneity and mischievous looks from the children make us see the journey in a new light. No matter the nationality, the culture, or the religion, and in whatever language, children have the power to give a new sense to life. From a coffee at a rest stop to a diabolo show, and from a meal in a restaurant overlooking the ocean to a surprise visit to the Mohammed Hassan II mosque in Casablanca, we live at the rhythm of this adorable family that gives us all their time and their attention. This is a true lesson in kindness that we appreciate deeply.

On the road between Casablanca and Kenitra, north of Rabat, we experience a different sort of ambiance in our next car, where we dance with Reda and Saad. The two young students play the amateur DJ role to make us vibrate to the sound of the Moroccan musical scene, and they succeed.

Yasin is our last driver of the day. An actor and a member of the Parliament, and an avid lover of meeting people and new discoveries, he multiplies our experiences in Morocco. From Kenitra all the way to the very doors of Tangier, we talk about his citizen engagement, his origins in the Chefchaouen province, and the artistic environment in which he'd like to spend more time.

Our trip from Marrakesh to Tangier has been a rich and diverse journey, just as we like them.

Once we're in the port city, we set off in fulfilling our second goal for the day: finding a place to stay for the night. The darkness reduces our field of vision, and the rain our field of action. Nonetheless, we bump into Zineb at the entrance of a general store. The young student amaze us with the energy she devotes to helping us find aid, and this attitude surprises as much as it delights us. Unfortunately, the family that she contacts can't host us, and Zineb is the first to be disappointed.

At 11 PM we still haven't found a place to stay. We are drenched to the bone, the shops are all closing, and we haven't the faintest idea of where to go, when suddenly the light coming from a bakery catches our eye. The employees are about to close the place and we discuss with them as they lock up and pull down the metal mesh in front of the doors. Mustafa, the young server, doesn't speak but a few words of French, but as soon as he understands that we are homeless for the night, he invites us to stay at his place.

Short of breath and still trembling but relieved, we arrive at his apartment. On the corner of the street we have a rather terrifying encounter that makes us jump and run for our lives. It's not, fortunately, every day that one runs into a masked man, armed with a menacing machete, while walking across a dark alley...

More scared than hurt, we follow Mustafa into his apartment. The building is occupied by a dozen young men, all of them visibly living on a dime. We climb the steps until we reach Mustafa's floor. The ambiance is peculir, with wisps of a smoke coming from an unknown substance penetrating the halls and tired faces looking out, but nonetheless the environment is convivial. Upon reaching the third floor, Mustafa shows us his room, where, on the floor, there are sheets acting as mattresses. We set down our backpacks and we join our hosts to eat a snack. We can see that, evidently, hospitality isn't dependent on means.

Day 77 – Monday, November 24th, 2014
Tangier, Morocco – Bilbao, Spain

It is still dark out when we leave Mustafa's apartment. The young man wakes up very early and we accompany him to his workplace. We help him set up the dining hall and the shop in exchange for breakfast, and then we head in the direction of the Port of Tangier.

There, the ferry companies show us the current prices for the journey across the sea. We are surprised at the elevated price of the tickets, even though we are in low season! The situation gets more complicated, and Europe, so close by, seems very far away to us.

Luckily, one of the employees gives us a helpful tip that replenishes our hopes: if we find a car to ride in, the driver won't have any additional fees to carry us with him. This is a true godsend!

It is Monday, so cars going by are rare. We keep our spirits high, though, because waiting is a part of our adventure and is often followed by success. Fortunately, the rule is confirmed and we joyfully get on the ferry heading to Tarifa, in Spain.

As the Moroccan coasts fade away behind us, the Strait of Gibraltar appears in the horizon and the sea, peaceful, is full of scintillating reflections. The environment on the ferry is relaxed in the beginning of the week, and Nadia, a member of the crew, opens the doors of the command post for us. There, the captain lets us sit in his seat, and this is a moment that is enough to revive our childhood dreams!

Finally, we reach Spain. The final stretch before Paris. Milan is delighted at the idea of being able to perfect his Spanish in the company of the people we will meet here. Thanks to Carla and Mohamed, whom we met during the ferry trip across the sea, the rest of the challenge quickly nears its end. We don't reach Madrid this night, as we had expected, we do even better: we reach Bilbao, in the north of the country. A trip of more than 1000 kilometers, done in one day, and we feel like we have wings.

We arrive after midnight in the city, and we don't even have to look for a place to stay, since Mohamed hosts us in his apartment and introduces us to his roommates, Idir, Youssef, and Mohammed. Today has been one of the easiest days that we've had during this adventure. We've had days with, days without, some highs, and some lows; we need a little bit of everything to make a journey around the world.

Day 78 – Tuesday, November 25th, 2014
Bilbao, Spain – Bordeaux, France

Motivated by the incredible distance traveled yesterday, we wake up feeling enthusiastic about our day to come. After having breakfast in the apartment, we follow Youssef and Mohammed through the streets of Bilbao. The city wakes up slowly as the students head to their schools and the shopkeepers open their boutiques.

The beginning of today's travels is a little chaotic. We face many difficulties finding tickets to go to the bus station, and then finding bus tickets. Nonetheless, at the beginning of the afternoon, and thanks to the help of many people, coin by coin and euro by euro, we finally depart the city, heading to San Sebastian.

At 4 in the afternoon, we start hitchhiking. We had been warned that this way of traveling wasn't the most effective in Spain, but we don't let ourselves be defeated. Isty, a charming Spanish woman, contradicts the wagging tongues. Her energy is contagious, and her humor charms us. With her, we easily ride all the way to the close-by border, and then to Hendaye, all without a hitch. After everything we've lived, we had forgotten about Europe and its principle of free movement!

Filled with joy at finally being back in France, we seized by the sudden desire to celebrate the present moment. We enter a bar to have a coffee and we share the news with Daniel, the bartender.

"France? That's after Bayonne. Here, we're in Basque Country!" he jokes.

191

Isty, who is of Spanish Basque origin, can't help but smile.

We talk for a while, and then Lucas, the 10-year-old nephew of an employee, joins us when he hears our story. Witnessing the marveled expression of a child when discovering an adventure has no price!

When the time comes to leave, we thank our new friends for the impromptu reception and we ride with Isty until we reach the tollgates on the highway in the direction of Bordeaux. There, cars drive past us without paying any sort of attention to our predicament, and the situation seems delicate. We are thrilled when, after an exceptionally long wait, a car stops and picks us up. We are so relieved to finally be able to move that we forget to ask about where we'll be dropped off, and this is how we find ourselves at a roundabout in the outskirts of Bayonne, one of the least strategic places to hitchhike that we have found. It is clear to see that there are still lonely moments to be lived after 78 days of travel...

After an hour of attempts, we succeed in getting driven to another tollbooth. There, the refusals continue until Benoît, a young banker, accepts to take us to the next rest stop. He has one condition, though: we must make a detour to pick up his young son before we go. We accept. Once at the rest stop, however, we begin to worry as it gets later and later. The parked Spanish cargo trailers aren't heading out any time soon and cars are rare. Finally, Bernard saves us from an unending wait, and two hours later, we discover the illuminated quays of the Girondin capital.

Bordeaux: we have reached the goal of our day.

Romain, a young student who has followed our adventure from the first day on our social media sites, immediately contacted us once he learned that one of the legs of our journey would bring us to his city. We accept the young man's invitation to stay at his place and we set up a meeting place in the city. He joins us, accompanied by his cousins Aymeric and Laurent, in the center of the city. Flattered to see that our initiative can have a positive impact on someone, we are delighted to be able to spend some time with them. We have a festive evening, light and happy, and full of cultural and culinary discoveries.

Bordeaux is truly deserving of its place in the path of Optimistic Traveler.

Day 79 – Wednesday, November 26th, 2014
Bordeaux – Paris, France

Our impatience and excitement wake us up early the next day, even though we haven't slept much. We are only a few hundred kilometers from the finish line, just a tiny fraction of the distance that we have traveled so far. Romain, making sure that we're prepared for the journey, gives us some indications to allow to easily leave the city and drives us to the tram stop. He holds out two tickets, happy to be able to contribute to this final stage of our journey.

We traverse the center of Bordeaux by public transport and we reach the outskirts where we practice our favorite daily game: hitchhiking. Same players, same rules, and we wait patiently to draw an ace in order to advance. It is Jean-Michel, a man of Italian descent living in Marseille, who is the first to pick us up. His Southern French accent lights up the gray morning and he accompanies us to the first service station on the highway heading to Paris, even though he must take a detour to do so. Romain, a banker and experienced hiker, crazy about travels and Norway, then advances us to Poitiers in a relaxed and pleasant ambiance. From there, we continue on with Youssef to Tours, and then with Sylvie and Hichem to Verneuil-sur-Seine, in the Parisian region. Our plan changes at the last minute, though, and we find ourselves on the peripheral boulevard, ready to pass by the doors of the capital.

The tip of the Eiffel Tower is visible over the skyline of buildings, and we can't believe our eyes. Still in the car, we can't stay still. Once we arrive on the Champs-Elysées, we let our joy explode in front of the dumbstruck and amazed eyes of Hichem and Sylvie.

After seventy-nine days of traveling, and twenty-four hours in advance, we are back in Paris.

The emotion is immense. The countries, the faces, the tests, the surprises... everything swirls around in our minds. We have seen and lived so many unimaginable things that make the experience seem almost surreal, and our arrival in Paris doesn't help us come down from our little cloud...

In the spirit of spicing up the evening and concluding our trek in a beautiful way, we call out to our community. All sorts of challenges soon start to pour in, such as traveling the last kilometers that separate us from the Eiffel Tower by bike. Another more improbable one seems to be unanimous on the web, and it is this last one that comes true before our very eyes. We don't know by what sort of miracle, but we find ourselves on the line with Antoine de Maximy. In Paris for a short while, the journalist that came up with and directed the groundbreaking travel show "J'irai dormir chez vous" ("I'll come sleep in your house"), invites us to... sleep in his house. An incredible twist of fate.

Supplied with his address, and with a beating heart, we set off on our last adventure. Following the advice of our host, a fervent supporter of the saying "the more the merrier", we bring with us Zelda and Diane, two young Parisian women with a striking sense of humor, whom we crossed during our trip across the city, and then Jenifer and Safa. Finally, at the end of an impasse, Antoine de Maximy, in the flesh, greets us. One of his friends, a dreamer and inventor by the name of Jean-Pierre, also joins our group. All of us, together, proceed to spend an evening to be remembered.

Direct and frank, simply and funny, Antoine shares his experiences as a seasoned and passionate traveler. He recognizes that we are not the first to ask to stay at his place, and he amusedly shares with us the reason why he agreed:

"In Hollywood, George Clooney refused to host me. Keeping everything in proportion, when I heard that you had just arrived in Paris after eighty days of challenges, I thought that an unexpected ending would be good for you!"

And he adds:

"What I love are the moments where something pleasant happens, where there's a sort of magic being created. Like tonight, here, all of us together."

We continue to talk in this festive ambiance and we share the most important aspects and moments of our journey. Everyone agrees that the generosity we were shown and benefited from was impressive. Antoine de Maximy made a special point to talk about our optimism:

"You knew to talk to people, and you knew how to be different characters. The contact was established and the success followed soon after. But, if the world was this perfect, there wouldn't be people sleeping in the street every night."

The presenter shows us here, with sincerity and humility, his way of thinking. The messages? They are too little for him; a legitimate and firm stance that dictates his way of traveling.

A good attitude and an openness to others, this is what leads to encounters, to sharing. And to evenings like these...

Day 80 – Thursday, November 27th, 2014
Paris, France

Last morning in our 80 Days Challenge. After a cup of coffee, we say goodbye to our out-of-the-ordinary host, thanking him warmly.

The day we have in front of us is nothing like the seventy-nine that preceded it. We are in no rush to travel hundreds of kilometers, and there is no hitchhiking to do. We still, however, have one last challenge that makes us feel a little heartache: we still have to find a place to stay tonight, in order to honor our rendezvous tomorrow morning, in front of the Eiffel Tower.

In between two professional meetings and reunions with friends, we run into an irresistible and elegant couple in a Parisian brasserie. We strike up a conversation, and Valeria and Didier, accustomed to the endless traffic passing through their house, respond positively without hesitation to our proposal. They have one condition, though, to allow us to have a roof over our heads for the night: we must cook dinner! We solve the situation with a slight compromise on our part: we will find someone to do the cooking tonight, and it is Severine, the owner of a leatherwork boutique, who will volunteer to play the part of chef.

The evening unfolds beautifully in a sublime architect-designed house – both Valeria and Didier exercise this profession – of the Nineteenth Arrondissement of Paris. Their children, Jules, 20, and Marie-Jeanne, 10 months, are also present. Camille, Severine's daughter, Évelyne, Georges, and Léa, our favorite team from Boulevard des Productions who has supported us throughout this whole journey, join our joyful group, as well.

The anecdotes flow freely, and travel and cultural differences have the place of honor given the Argentinean origin of our hostess. The ambiance is festive, the plates are full, and the table, lively and boisterous, is worthy of a family reunion. After eighty days on the road, we feel full and satisfied.

A beautiful conclusion to this extraordinary human adventure.

BACK
TO
PARIS

80 DAYS = 46 793KM

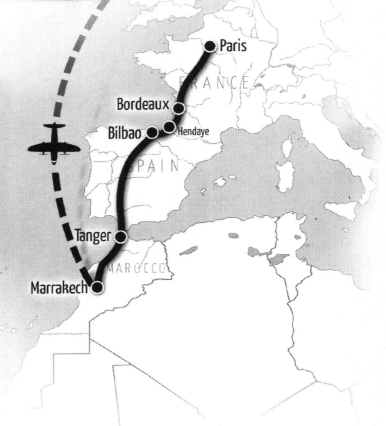

Paris

FRANCE

Bordeaux

Bilbao ● Hendaye

SPAIN

Tanger

MOROCCO

Marrakech

Conclusion

Friday, November 28th, 2014
Paris, France, 9 AM

At the end of the 47,000 kilometers, nineteen countries, and four continents we have traveled across, we determinedly and happily walk toward our last goal, the Eiffel Tower. We are short of breath, and our legs are jittery, but the smiles never leave our faces, and represent our joy at accomplishing this challenge.

This adventure was not an ordinary voyage: the idea of leaving with only a desire to travel across a large number of countries in a short amount of time was far from our heads. We set specific rules and a frantic race followed. In the heat of the moment, we developed a synergy – sometimes opposite, sometimes similar behaviors – that created this ardor and dynamism unique to our duo, at least according to the statements we heard during the significant and constructive encounters that led to reflection and self-questioning. Encounters that were either spontaneous or sought-after, but always oriented by the same aspiration.

We wanted the challenge to be extraordinary, and it unfolded as such. With the help of all of the people that we met along the way, we accomplished our mission. The circle is complete, and we return to the arches of the Iron Lady and the faces of the people who aided us during the voyage. Family, friends, and also some people that we didn't expect to see peeking out of the crowd, such as Sybille, who met us at the UN in New York City, or Christiane, who bought us plane tickets to Marrakesh and whom we're finally meeting. The emotions we feel are tangible.

In the course of our days of travel, we saw our ideas expand and wishes grow. Getting involved, helping, and sharing: there is still so much to do to keep up the momentum. We are back in Paris, rich with each experience that we lived, and yet, we haven't gained a single material benefit from this adventure. Our backpacks are as light as they were at the beginning of our journey, even though their contents fluctuated throughout the eighty days. We were effectively able to adapt with ease to the vastly different climates thanks to exchanges and to clothing donations. In this spirit, we gave away every one of the presents we received from hosts; a natural gesture to mark our gratitude.

Friday, December 5th, 2014
Provins, France. Jules Verne School

The path continues even after this first challenge is over. A path that leads us, one week after our arrival, to a school in the Parisian region. The name Jules Verne finally appeared in the Optimistic Traveler experience after a poignant letter from a teacher:

"While listening to the radio on this morning of September 9th, and being completely unmoved by the monotone flow of news, a little ray of optimism perked my ears. Two young men had taken upon the crazy challenge to travel across the world without money, upon the principle that the world's inhabitants could show generosity and solidarity.

I kept this piece of news in the corner of my head, envious of Muammer and Milan's audacity, and questioned myself about the plausibility of such a project...

The school year soon began. A teacher in special needs education in a school in Seine-et-Marne, I was taking charge of a new class of sixth-grade students.

My students... children from numerous disadvantaged places where education was at the same time advantageous and secondary...

Children that have already been thrown aside by life and in whom I want to give a desire: a desire to read, to discover, to learn, to share, to reflect, and to create...

A long and non-exhaustive list that I can't fulfill if I don't punctuate it with fun and interesting projects that are the key to success in my profession.

I explained to my students the functioning of the school, the Jules Verne School, named after the famous writer, author of the famous Around the World in Eighty Days. Together, we flipped through a copy of the book that I had in the bookcase in the back of the classroom. We discovered that an American journalist of that time, Nellie Bly, had herself undertaken this journey around the world in seventy-two days, and that she had, during this trip, met Jules Verne.

It was then that I told them what I had heard that morning on the radio: the men of Optimistic Traveler had taken upon themselves an ambitious trek, reproducing the one that Phileas Fogg and Jean Passepartout had completed two centuries before.

I knew that I had my first interesting project when I saw the eyes of Nadège, Maëva, Kévin, Mikail, Jason, Kentigern, Julie, Camille, Clara, Ethan, Romaric, and Brian shine with curiosity...

These were children who had, for the most part, never traveled anywhere, and to whom a trip to the cinema was already an extraordinary event in their often difficult lives, and they were fascinated with this slightly wild enterprise around the world with only a good mood and optimism as baggage. Of course, when one has nothing and lives it every day, seeing others do big things represents much more than a brave challenge.

Phileas Fogg wanted to move with the times while profiting from the industrial revolution, and Muammer and Milan were going to similarly go against the common values of their era, money and individualism.

The Optimistic Travelers added a singular difficulty to their trip by traveling without money to prove, as they say, that there are good people in the world.

Challenge set! Students motivated!

It was in this way that, day after day, we followed the trek of the two travelers. The students marked, on the wall of the classroom, the map of Europe with a first Post-It on the city of Paris, France, with a date of September 9th written on it.

Soon after, the yellow labels multiplied, creating a beautiful garland, and we annotated each date, each place, and each stage of the journey. Afterwards, it was evident that we needed to switch maps to one of the globe since, as if it was the easiest thing in the world, our travelers were blazing quite a trail!

The students lived each stage with joy, nervousness, and sometimes even with anguish when Muammer and Milan were stuck at the Iranian border without their papers. The time went by and they were still in the same country, unable to move forward and wasting time in their challenge. Were they going to be able to succeed in making it across the world in the time they had established?

Every day, at the end of the French lesson, we checked up on the advancement of the globetrotters by reading the articles on the internet. Mikail, of Turkish origin, translated the messages written in his native language, which stirred up the admiration of his classmates. In a similar fashion to an advent calendar, reading the chronicles of this voyage day after day was like opening a surprise piece of chocolate that is discovered with impatience.

The students were enthusiastic upon reading about each encounter and each show of solidarity. They shared Muammer and Milan's adventures as if they were holding their hands throughout their journey.

On Friday, November 28th, 2014, eighty days after the beginning of their optimistic challenge, Muammer and Milan reached the Eiffel Tower, thanks to the generosity of people all over the world.

100 kilometers from there, in a small-town, twelve sixth-grade students followed the steps of the two friends, hearts beating, and with their minds full of images...

The journey around the world was shared, and it was there that the challenge was conquered!

-Madame, do you think that we could also meet Muammer and Milan, since they've already given so much to so many people?" Mikail asked me yesterday...

Challenge accepted!"

Sandie Masson.

Becoming, in the eyes of this group of children, "optimistic explorers" as they've named us, and showing them a way to open up to others is certainly one of the most beautiful rewards that we could have gained from this adventure...

February, 2015
Port-au-Prince, Haiti

We switch the freezing winter temperature in Europe for the tropical heat of Haiti. Thanks to our internet community and the media visibility brought about by this project, the fundraising campaign launched during the 80 Days Challenge was a success, so much so that we are able to use the money intelligently by aiding the Haiti Care association.

During a month, and by doing renovation work via creating a garden space, playing board games and sharing juggling lessons, and holding workshops on painting murals, we evolve within the contact of the children and adults of the MEVA School in Port-au-Prince. Under the tutelage of the founder, Michael Kaash, and his volunteers, the Optimistic Traveler team grows, and the magic that has followed us during this whole trip operates once again. As promised, Joe Miller joins us from Chicago. His art fascinates and marvels everyone, young and old, and its luminous colors brighten up the drab walls of the buildings. His intervention wins over everyone, crowns our first step toward humanitarianism, and comforts our desires.

The magic of the journey also allows us to relive this magnificent voyage through the pen of Gaëlle, whom we met on board the California Zephyr somewhere in the United States, between Utah and Colorado.
We witnessed multiple collaborations, the association of many talents, and many personalities that punctuated our Optimistic Traveler journey, all of which we hope will continue being numerous and relevant so that our new projects come to fruition.

We were born curious and adventurous, with a need to push against the limits, so that they no longer exist, and to be able to live a life full of freedom. Our childhood dreams remain with us always, something which, probably, makes us believe that people are generous, warm, tolerant, and able to open up to others. Our challenge confirmed all of our convictions and our hopes, but this is only the beginning.
We would love to say that anyone can do this challenge, but

this is unfortunately not true. We are conscious that our circumstances have been favorable to us. We are white men, citizens of the European Union, with passports and international health insurance, with family and friends who support us every step of the way, savings, a good education, pre-existing travel experience, media support...

Yes, there are good people everywhere, and it is thanks to their generosity that we were able to complete our challenge. Nonetheless, injustice and discrimination due to skin color, to gender, to political opinion, or to sexual orientation, continue to exist. Optimism is a great force and it can change many things, but it cannot beat prejudice. We, the Optimistic Travelers, want to help improve our world with your help.

Optimistic Traveler exists now more than ever. All the benefits and gifts that we receive are spent on good causes, such as the Haiti Care mission. We go to new countries where people need help. Our humanitarian dream is finally in action, but our desire to give back everything we've received is far from being satisfied.

We love the world and today we are going to change it!

The world is good, and there are good people everywhere!

It was our mission to prove this, and we have accomplished it! Without a penny in our pockets, we have succeeded, and this was thanks to the generosity of the world.

There are valuable lessons to be taken from each of the journeys and adventures people live throughout their lives. The challenges we face make up our lives and it is important to be aware of the new treasures we receive in order to move forward, grow, and help our fellow humans.

These eighty days gave us no choice but to face these lessons, even when that's what we wanted the most. The world, even with its differences, its darker parts, and its barriers, is good and generous. To help us detect this facet, that is often cast aside, and to see it last in the future, some guidelines are essential.

Humility, first.
The society in which we evolve in creates gaps and disparities that separate us, so we must remember that we were all born equals. The feeling of superiority tied to the privileges of a certain condition doesn't lead to anything but conflict. In

the face of delicate or difficult situations, perspective can put everything in its place: complaints should no longer exist, and humility should take their place.

Respect and tolerance, second.

Seeing people's good sides, chasing away prejudices, looking past appearances: each person, each entity, no matter who, is worthy of interest and possesses qualities. Tolerance leads to respect, and vice versa. The world deserves this sort of attention.

Altruism, third.

Caring about the well-being of others can be manifested in different ways. Offering time to others is a first step: it doesn't matter how much, what matters is the quality of this time; the relationships we form with our neighbors are the next step: looking upon the people that surround us with a loving and welcoming gaze can be nothing but beneficial; finally, pulling away or detaching oneself from the society of consumption that more often than not dictates our actions is yet another step, and far from the smallest. Being disinterested is the key: happiness does not reside in the material nor does it come from financial success.

These are all universal values that embellish any adventure, large and small, here and there.

Listening, observing, and learning; all of this leads to application. One must detach oneself from theory in order to pass to the practice...

Bon voyage,

Optimistic Traveler.

I HAVE A DREAM / AFRICA

19 dreams that can change lives...

Muammer and Milan are not finished with their adventures. At the end of 2016, after many action-packed weeks, they came back from their latest quest with their hearts full to the brim with emotions.

Discover "I HAVE A DREAM / AFRICA".

They traveled across Africa in 80 days with one mission: to make the dreams of people they met along the way come true. After having traveled across 7,000 kilometers and 7 different countries, the Optimistic Travelers made many of these become a reality:

- Planting trees in a school;
- Buying plane tickets for young people living in shanty towns;
- Accompanying an orphanage in their mission;
- Changing the roof of a grandmother's house;
- Buying wheelchairs for handicapped children so that they could see something else besides the walls of their own homes;
- Buying a sewing machine for a handicapped woman

and stay-at-home mother;
- Offering a free hot air balloon trip
... and thousands of smiles.

What did this Optimistic Traveler journey look like?
- Hitchhiking on African highways and meeting many incredible people;
- Sleeping in people's homes and sharing the life of the poorest, as well as the richest;
- Talking with everyone they cross, and meeting strangers that become friends;
- Giving several speeches in schools, at the Alliance Française, at fairs, and at the United Nations in Nairobi.

Everything is completely improvised because, more often than not, their arrival in a city or a country is carried out without a single contact, without booked lodging, and without any real preparation.

They have dedicated all of the funds gathered from this book you're holding between your hands to help realize the dreams they encountered, and they are now preparing a documentary film that retraces their steps across Africa.

Itinerary: South Africa, Botswana, Zimbabwe, Zambia, Tanzania, Kenya, and Ethiopia.

Optimistic Traveler
www.facebook.com/optimistictravel

Muammer Yilmaz and Milan Bihlmann
optimistictraveler@gmail.com

ACKNOWLEDGMENTS

BOULEVARD DES PRODUCTIONS

We were two on the road but a team, which was almost like a family, supported us. Thank you to Évelyne NOIRIEL, Georges PRATS, Léa, and the whole team at Boulevard des Productions that aided us every step of the way. Before the trip, they gifted us with ten memory cards with a 64-gigabyte capacity, as well as a microphone and some accessories. During our adventure, these were constantly present, from the creation of the website to the livestreams, the 80-second video shorts, and the social media platforms. Thank you.

http://www.boulevard.fr

TAMERA

Éric BONNEM and his whole team were our travel partners. Their knowledge of the world, their precious advice, and their visa sponsors were a huge help to us. Without them, it would have taken much longer to obtain the Iranian visa and it would have been practically impossible to cross Pakistan. They continue to support us at a distance... a huge thank you!

http://www.tamera.fr/fr

LEOGANT

The source of life, water, indispensable during each day of our journey. Thank you to the German technology and the

whole team at Leogant.
http://www.leogant.de/progress/

REAL TRANSPORT
Aziz SOYLU, the chief of this Turkish company, adored our project and bought us a plane ticket to cross the ocean.

IMAGIN
Hakim BENASSOUL supported us during this adventure, and he encouraged us to write a book in order to share our story with the world. Michel LAFON was our editor.
http://www.imagin-communication.info

MICHEL LAFON
In person, Michel is drawn to the energy of Optimistic Traveler. Not only did he edit our book, but he also promised us a donation of $7,300 to participate in our project to change the world with us, and to launch a new humanitarian project together!
http://www.michel-lafon.fr

LUDOVIC HUBLER
He traveled across the world in 80 days while hitchhiking, an extraordinary trip which is even better to live through in his book. He followed our adventure and gave us advice during our trip. http://www.ludovichubler.com/fr/

He recently launched the superb project Travel with a Mission, make sure to sign up!
http://www.travelwithamission.org/fr/

NOUVELLES FRONTIÈRES
Gaël PHALEMPIN, from Annecy, sponsored our trip to Haiti and will buy Muammer's plane ticket so that our donations go directly to children in need.
http://www.nouvelles-frontieres.fr

VIP STUDIO

We established a partnership with VIP Studio concerning the material of our filming. They lent us two cameras (GH3 and GH4), as well as three lens and ten 64-gigabyte memory cards. www.vip-prod.fr

KIM

A quiet force that deserves recognition. A companion during our everyday life that allowed us to build this project. A counselor like no other. Thank you for your patience. Thank you for being at our side. We love you!

FRANÇOIS KLAUTH

He surprised us and good-naturedly participated in our humanitarian project in Haiti!

LOTFY DIBAOUI

He accompanied us to Haiti, and even with the difficult conditions he managed to work with us there. His youth and his motivation helped us immensely. He has found a sponsor for his plane ticket, bravo!

BERNARD CANTOS

We met him on the Metz highway, where he picked us up with his beautiful Katie. We then spent twenty-four hours together; this is the magic of hitchhiking and human encounters.

TEAM

Thank you to our entourage, who from the shadows has advised, encouraged, and motivated us through each step of this adventure. Some of them helped learned about our itinerary, others participated in the translation, and yet others helped prepare the voyage with us.

Thank you to every person who helped us!

Optimistic Traveler

A human adventure full of love and emotion.
Carried out between September 9th and November 28th,
 2014

www.optimistic-traveler.com
optimistictraveler@gmail.com

Facebook:
www.facebook.com/optimistictravel

YouTube:
www.youtube.com/c/Optimistic Traveler

Instagram:
http://instagram.com/optimistictravel

Twitter:
https://twitter.com/OptimisticTrav

Muammer Yilmaz
www.muammer.fr
www.facebook.com/muammer.fr

Made in the USA
San Bernardino, CA
18 September 2018